Sacrifice and Delight

OTHER BOOKS BY ALAN JONES

Exploring Spiritual Direction

Journey into Christ

Living in the Spirit (coauthor)

Passion for Pilgrimage

Soul Making

Sacrifice and Delight

SPIRITUALITY

FOR MINISTRY

Alan Jones

HarperSanFrancisco

A Division of HarperCollins*Publishers*

FIRST EDITION

Library of Congress Cataloging-in-Publication Data

Jones, Alan W.
   Sacrifice and delight: spirituality for ministry / Alan Jones.—1st ed.
     p. cm.
   Includes bibliographical references.
   ISBN 0–06–064213–0 (alk. paper)
   1. Clergy—Religious life. 2. Clergy—Office. 3. Jones, Alan W.
  4. Anglican Communion—Clergy—Biography. 5. Clergy—
Psychology. I. Title.
BV4011.6.J66   1992
253′.2—dc20   91–55419
                                          CIP

92 93 94 95 96 BG 10 9 8 7 6 5 4 3 2 1

This edition is printed on acid-free paper that meets the American National Standards Institute Z39.48 Standard.

In memoriam
Rachel Hosmer, O.S.H.
Hugh Bishop

In thanksgiving
Jim, Michael, Lauren and Marc, Fred, Philip and Bill

For my School of Love
Josephine, Lena, Charlotte, Edward

Contents

Preface

My life in faith is a cycle of sacrifice and delight. In this book I try to describe something of that cycle, both in my own life and in the lives of those who are ordained, in the hope that it will touch the lives of any who try to follow Christ. Sacrifice is essentially a creative and nurturing act. Raimundo Panikkar puts it well:

> Sacrifice is at the center of the world, its force, that which gives it the strength to be, to be what it is and what it shall be, that which supports the cosmos and maintains it in existence. Sacrifice is not primarily a human affair but a cosmic venture, and God and the Gods are the prime actors in it. Sacrifice is not only the creative act, it is also both conservational and the actively transforming act of the whole universe.[1]

The purpose of sacrifice *is* delight. It is a mistake, perhaps, to think about sacrifice *and* delight. Rather, sacrifice is for the sake of delight. God went out of himself, risked himself, out of sheer delight to create the world. From the point of view of the cosmic venture, there is no delight without such sacrificial risk.

I see all human beings (all being) invited into the cosmic venture—the cosmic adventure of sacrifice for the sake of delight. That invitation is also at the heart of the ordained ministry.

A Love Letter and Survival Manual

What follows is not only a highly personal statement about the ordained ministry but also a kind of love letter to my fellow ministers of all denominations, who have supported me along the way. I know many priests and pastors from the various traditions, and in spite of historical and theological differences, our struggles and hopes are much the same. We all seek to be obedient to the call of Christ and we all, one way or another, fail. On some level, clergy cannot possibly practice what they preach. Those who think they do are a menace to themselves and others. Yet God works through us, and people are touched, lives are changed.

I am continually amazed by the way lives are turned around by simple "unintended" acts. People I have never met write to say that their lives have been changed by something I have written, and I wonder how it could have happened. Something that I scarcely understand is always going on between people. The way we interact with one another fills me with wonder.

This book is also something of a survival manual—my attempt to speak to the conditions and terms of the minister's life and to interpret our lives as a cycle of sacrifice and delight as we approach the end of the millennium. The ordained need help to serve in a culture that reduces religion to a leisure-time pursuit for individuals who use it to cope with the stresses and strains of the present time but do not see it as important beyond the personal and private. Insofar as this is true, my experience of ministry has been of swimming against the current. I do not always go with the flow. I find that our resistance to the delight at the heart of things is as strong as our resistance to sacrifice, because we do not understand that sacrifice and delight are ways of talking about the same thing.

A book about ministry, and about the ordained ministry in particular, seen through the eyes of a particular man may seem narrowly conceived. From one point of view, it is. Christianity is only one religion among many, and thousands of people claim no particular faith. The ordained, after all, constitute but a small subculture within a particular religious system. To make things more difficult, among Christians there are conflicting views on the meaning and function of the ordained. Yet the implications of this book reach far beyond the bounds of a particular religion, and certainly beyond the interests of those who happen to be ordained. Why? Because a religious perspective provides a prism through which we can look at the world. In writing this book I think not only of the ordained but all who want to understand their culture and themselves a little better.

Priest, Minister, Pastor

The reader may find it odd at best, and irritating at worst, that I make no attempt to distinguish between the words *priest, minister,* and *pastor.* If I were writing a theological treatise on ecclesiology and church polity, distinguishing between these words would be important. My focus, however, is on the person of the minister. My concerns are spiritual and psychological. My prejudice is, however, that theology has long since drifted away from its spiritual and psychological moorings and needs grounding once again in human experience.

Thanks

Books don't just happen. My thanks are due to St. John's Roman Catholic Seminary in Camarillo, California, where I was asked to give an anniversary lecture on the priesthood, and to the trustees who invited me to give the annual Eric Abbott Memorial Lecture in Westminster Abbey in London. Such gracious invitations were the stimuli I needed to write a "love letter."

Writing requires time, space, and solitude, and I am grateful to the friends at El Rancho del Obispo in Healdsburg, California, for their hospitality. My editors (John Shopp, Roland Seboldt, and Ronald Klug) have been wonderfully patient and supportive. Finally there are my "priestly" colleagues (unordained and ordained) at Grace Cathedral, San Francisco, who have taught me more about the romance of ministry than I can ever express.

Sacrifice and Delight

CHAPTER ONE

Broken Humanity: God's Instruments for Ministry

M y vision of the ordained person is that of a lover in a mad love affair. I realize that this sounds romantic and naive, particularly in a culture that cannot cope with the erotic in religion. My view of love is neither sentimental nor naive, but it is romantic. Love is demanding as well as gentle; tough as well as tender; blazing with the fire of judgment as well as brimming over with the oil of healing and forgiveness. How can anyone make a profession of being a bearer of love when no one loves consistently and well all the time? It is a question of playing a role.

Learning to love the role without overidentifying with it is one of the most challenging tasks of the minister. Some wear their personas like a suit of armor they never take off. Others treat their personas like an old overcoat to be worn when necessary but taken off from time to time. In this respect, ministers are like actors. We have to play a role, but we get into a mess when we cannot set the role aside. The trick is how to love the role without letting it take you over. In 1944 Laurence Olivier was playing the part of Sergius in George Bernard Shaw's play *Arms and the Man*. It wasn't going well. The director, Tyrone Guthrie, asked Olivier, "Don't you love Sergius?" The actor confessed that he didn't. "Well, if you can't love him, you'll never be any good in him, will you?" Without loving our role we will not be good in it.

1

The Christian ministry has all the ups and downs of a love affair. I come by the image honestly. The mystics viewed Christianity as the "School of Love" and were unafraid to use the imagery of romance. Many Christians seem to spend all their energy seeing to it that no hint of romance is left. The actor Alec Guinness writes that soon after his reception into the Roman Catholic Church, he found himself running, like a lover, down a London street simply to find a church where he could spend a few minutes in the presence of the reserved sacrament.[1] This gesture of love is in stark contrast to Carl Jung's description of his first communion. He observed that the people returned from receiving the sacrament solemn and lifeless. To them the idea of romance would have been considered blasphemous.

Lovers and Sinners

Much of the romance and passion seem to have gone out of life in general as well as out of Christianity. Are their only vestiges the erotic scandals surrounding some ordained ministers? Or is there something here worth exploring? Since I am a lover, I am also a sinner: a sinner because no one loves clearly and perfectly. The words *sin* and *sinner* are unfamiliar or unclear to many people nowadays. Like the word *God,* sin is one of the polluted and lost words in our vocabulary. This can make life difficult for the ordained, because these are essential words in the basic phrase book of religion.

Anyone who tries to love knows what it is to sin. There are no perfect lovers, and sin is the failure to love. Lovers know about betrayal and forgiveness, and to be ordained is to be exposed to love, betrayal, and forgiveness in a peculiar way.

Is it any wonder that many of us fail, drink too much, get morally confused, and suffer from depression? Is it any wonder that those who take on a symbolic role for and in society should feel isolated and occasionally crushed by it? Is it any wonder that of all groups I know, the clergy seems to be the most resistant to spiritual and psychological growth? The clergy, by their profession, are supposed to know about love, sin, and forgiveness firsthand. Admitting ignorance of the very things they are being "paid" to profess, therefore, is very difficult for them.

I am a sinner who believes that love and goodness are at the heart of things. I am neither proud of being a sinner nor crippled by the knowledge of my failure to love. I have a profound respect for psychotherapy and have been through various forms of counseling that were life-bearing and healing. But I have been hurt by the way my own sinning and that of my fellow pastors has been caricatured by psychological reductionisms, by such things as the codependency movement (which has much to teach us but is not the last word). A human being is deeply hurt when he or she is seen as only a set of problems and not as an unfathomable mystery. The overriding metaphor for the sickness of society is that of addiction. But the metaphor is overdone. We are an addicted people, but that is not all we are.

We love explanations, but human longings (romance again) cannot be explained away. We reduce and diminish each other with partial and distorted descriptions masquerading as explanations. We say such things as, "She's neurotic," and "He's compulsive." We think we've solved a problem by naming a person an alcoholic or an adult child of one. Naming things is important, but damage is done when we presume to name a part for the whole. We label people and problems with such conviction that we really begin to believe that we have explained someone away.

To be ordained is to rage against these reductions and diminishments. Our longing and our sinning are often reduced by cheap psychologizing to images of maladjustment. It's not that there aren't issues of addiction and codependence for all of us. But there is more to us than these. And it is to this "more" that I wish to speak. I call that "more" the romance of ministry. What then of my own romance?

Romance

I see my life in general and my vocation in particular as one long romance, in style caught somewhere between a paperback love story and something solid and grand on the scale of Dante's *Divine Comedy*. The absurdities of the former and the deep longings of the latter are with me all the time, as a man and as a priest. I must confess that my vocation is still something of a mystery to me. I have always been a somewhat reluctant believer, partly out of embarrassment and snobbery with regard to my fellow believers and partly because of the daring enormity of our beliefs.

I don't take easily to Christianity, because, on one level, it simply doesn't "work." Christians, in my experience, do not behave more compassionately than others. Its ministers are a mixed group. Many are deeply wounded, some are predatory. Believing, therefore, doesn't come to me "naturally" the way it seems to come to some people.

But I don't want to give the impression that it's all uphill. There is delight at the center too. It's just that some people seem to be naturally and spontaneously "good" (and not in a goody-goody way), while others aren't. I'm one of those people who have to work at believing and at being "good." While I don't think of myself as particularly "bad," the simple truth is that spiritually speaking I see myself as a very slow learner. I have grown into being a Christian very slowly. Being a minister has been one of the ways in which I have grown into who I am. That's why my spiritual life, such as it is, is characterized by a sense of wonder and newness. I wake up in the morning surprised that I have been given another day to see if I can "get it right."

My vocation descended on me when I was only fifteen. It didn't come to me as a glowing feeling to serve or to help people. It was, rather, like a toothache that wouldn't go away—a persistent pain, an attraction to the crucified Savior that no doubt would have been thought of as neurotic and unhealthy had I been able at the time to articulate my feelings to a therapist. I was drawn, amazed, by the divine love that would go to such lengths for me. I believe God was and is in my call to be a priest. I am genuinely mystified about why God would choose me for this particular calling. I am glad to be ordained, and I feel very blessed to be a minister of Christ. But being ordained has also been a struggle.

Staying Christian and a Priest

One Christmas my family was given a holiday treat—a cruise along the Mexican Riviera from Los Angeles to Acapulco. We sailed on a British ship a few days after Christmas. On a Sunday during the trip I attended the interdenominational service led by the captain. I think he had confused the service with the burial office. There was no mention of Christmas. There were just a few prayers from the English Book of Common

Prayer of 1662, and we sang all the stanzas of "Onward Christian Sol-
diers." I felt that I had wandered into a Monty Python sketch—an echo
of what might have once been a religion. I was even a little ashamed of
being ordained.

But the congregation didn't seem to notice or mind. I was the only
one who seemed enraged or disappointed. My wife had warned me not
to go. (She knows me better than I know myself, and she knew what it
would be like.) I left chastened and angry. It made me wonder what it
was that kept me in the Church at all. Why bother with it? I felt like one
of Iris Murdoch's lapsed priests—like someone who had ceased to bother
yet wanted to try again. As one of her fictional clergymen puts it, "I may
even try to creep back into some cranny in the Anglican church when
the theologians have dismantled it all a bit more."[2] I would add, "And
when the psychoanalysts and the mystics have made it more honest."

The biggest stumbling block to my belief has always been other
people, yet my believing (such as it is) rests on the graciousness of others.
I am grateful to a large number of people who made me and keep me a
believer and who saw something in me that I couldn't see in myself. I
have come to a point in my life when I need to acknowledge the debt I
owe to those who went on believing in me when I could no longer believe
in myself. My assumption is that if I try to work my way through some
tangled thoughts and feelings about how I stay a Christian and a priest,
I might speak to some of my brothers and sisters who live the strange life
of the ordained. Like Jean Sulivan, "I write to lie a little less."[3]

Telling My Story

God deals in particularities and works through individual people
with their own peculiar histories, their own unique sensibilities. I believe
that particularities (what makes you you and me me) are fraught with
universal significance. I believe that there is genuine divine commerce
between persons. If I tell something of my story, therefore, it is with the
conviction that it will in some way make a connection with yours precisely because there is a larger Story that unites us all. This has been my
experience in many of my encounters with others. Men and women (some
still living, many dead) have shared with me something of their story of
faith and helped me to understand my own. I have been helped by those

I would call saints, who have made me who I am by setting my life in a far larger context or narrative than I could have imagined on my own. In short, I have been formed by those who saw something in me to love.

The truth about ourselves is always elusive. Thus I would not claim that what I write here about myself and my experience as an ordained minister is "true." It is simply the best I can do with what I have. Perhaps by telling it, I shall learn to lie a little less.

The England of 1940–60 made me and in some ways hurt me, yet I am grateful. The Church of England (stuffy, self-satisfied, and yet sometimes wonderfully generous), through some of its diverse adherents, formed me as a Christian and as a pastor. I began in an evangelical Sunday school and was trained for the priesthood in an Anglo-Catholic theological college. The great thing about the Church of England of my youth was that one could run the whole gamut of the ecumenical scene and still remain an Anglican. This background has made me deeply sympathetic to the ordained of all denominations. I see in all of us common aspirations, needs, and problems.

A Generous Vision of Christianity—
Catholicity

One who helped me to understand myself was an Anglican monk. Herbert Kelly was born in 1860 and died in 1950. What attracted me to him was his generous vision of Christianity. *Catholicity,* he called it, in opposition to Catholic*ism* (which in this context we might call Christian*ism*). He meant not Roman Catholicism but any form of Christianity that claimed to have the mystery of God all buttoned up. Kelly hated *isms* of any kind. There are those for whom religion provides all the answers, and there are those for whom the answers, as important as they are, only lead to deeper and more disturbing questions. Kelly was of the latter school, and so am I.

Kelly taught me that only God is "Catholic" and that the Catholic church hasn't happened yet. This was a liberating lesson to learn in the midst of the rigid and class-conscious Christianity of my youth. I have become the kind of "Catholic" Christian who is at home with his "Protestant" brothers and sisters (if they will have him!) and for whom labels and parties are diminishing and hurtful.

Kelly taught me the importance of thinking for myself and of being able to tell the difference between my thoughts and my obsessions. He also taught me to be unafraid of passion in religion.

In the middle of the terrible agony of the First World War (October 1917), Kelly wrote:

> I want persecution. I want a few bishops shot against a wall. Priests in crowds. . . . You'd be astonished if you knew *how* serious I was in saying that. "Without the shedding of blood there is no remission of sins." Least of all sins like ours. The sins of "patronage" cry to heaven for vengeance. The sins of gentlemanliness, the sins of professionalism, the sins of smugness and comfort. . . . Mere disestablishment might do some good, but not much. You see it would leave all the dignitaries and professors, all the old gang, with their vested interests, to reorganize, as near as might be, where they were before. . . . I would gladly leave the Dissenters *their* endowments, *and* ours, Churches, Cathedrals, Vicarages, and we—what was left of us— would walk out in to the streets and talk about God.[4]

Kelly was struggling with an issue that is always with us. The Christianity of his day was so identified with the contemporary culture that the spirit was in danger of suffocating. The Church of England was too safe, too comfortable. Kelly thought that it had lost its way. Something drastic was called for.

Inner and Outer Revolution

From Kelly I learned of the Christian's continual inner revolution. Outwardly I tend to be a conformist and uncomfortable with revolutionary gestures. I agree with Kelly. Revolution tends to be a way for the same old gang to regroup under another name.

Readers need to know this about me because they will find little in these pages directly about revolution or even about the passion for justice. How dare I admit this? Because although a concern for justice is central to my faith, I find it best to come at these things passionately but obliquely, since it is my experience that the people who scream the loudest about justice often act unjustly. I have come across peace groups chiefly known for their belligerence, and (among the clergy) neurotic and even pathological behavior often masquerading as "prophetic" action.

I ask readers (particularly those who see themselves as activists) to be patient with me. We need each other. Simon the Zealot and Matthew the tax collector were both disciples of Jesus. One might have been called a terrorist, the other, a collaborator; but they both found themselves following Christ. More and more I see this as a matter of the different roles people are called to play in the life of the world. Some are called to break down; others are called to build up.

History Contaminates Everything

Being a pastor and trying to be a Christian have convinced me of two things. First, religious truth (any truth that really matters) comes to us in symbolic form. One can't look at it as if it were a bare and simple fact. Things that matter to us are severely distorted when we view them with a literalist squint. Second, history "contaminates" everything. There is no pure form. Because of this, our faith demands hard thinking.

Many ministers are intellectually underprepared. Still less are we ready to go through personal pain to the point where psychological, spiritual, and theological truths coincide in one grace-filled moment. We try to dodge this path by jumping on liberal or conservative bandwagons. For example, liberals are good at relativizing and even ridiculing the past but poor at doing the same thing to the present. Conservatives fail to understand that they are no less trapped in the spirit of some age or other even if it doesn't happen to be this one. In the middle of our confusion, many clergy are in deep personal pain, much of it faithless and unnecessary. Part of it is the refusal to face and to know ourselves.

Those who have helped form me have been unafraid to look inside themselves. They have been unafraid of a certain kind of pain. Americans are often accused by the English of being too "psychological," as indeed they are sometimes. Yet the English aren't or weren't "psychological" enough. It would do a great deal of good to subject some so-called theological statements to rigorous psychological analysis.

Self-knowledge shows us that we are not one but many selves. So it is with the forms of Christianity. Many of them and their various contents are sometimes disturbingly contradictory. As true and as obvious as this is, the clergy, in practice, often fail to take seriously Christianity's multiplicity and contradictions. Its many cultural manifestations are startling.

Culture and traditions make a difference. The Christianity of Texas in the 1990s isn't that of rural England of the last century. Both are in stark contrast, for example, to the Christianity of Lisbon in the eighteenth century. What do a contemporary Baptist minister, a nineteenth-century Anglican clergyman, and an eighteenth-century Portuguese Catholic priest have in common? The answer is, not much, except their culture-bound allegiance to "the little man on the cross." A long, hard look at the architecture of the churches of the various denominations should make one pause in claiming that Christianity has any one single, abiding content. God is One. We are legion.

With this in mind, I think of how the Englishness of the Christianity in which I was formed has affected me. I go back to when I was eight years old in the choir at St. Mary's, Wimbledon, in south London. When those middle-aged men in their three-piece suits, their watch chains draped across their bellies, read the Scripture lessons at high morning prayer, the Old Testament prophets sounded as if they had gone to minor but expensive private schools. In the England of my youth, being a Christian meant being a "good chap," and this had a specific cultural meaning.

God's Call to Transparency

The people who have influenced me most have been startlingly particular yet have transcended their peculiarities. Psychoanalyst James Hillman writes of the person who is transparent, of the one who knows firsthand the pain and the necessity of self-revelation, which is an act of love. Hillman wants us to shift our ideal from the *enlightened* person to the *transparent* one. Hillman does not mean the "Enlightened Man who sees, the seer, but the Transparent Man, who is seen and seen through, foolish, who has nothing left to hide, who has become transparent through self-acceptance; his soul is loved, wholly revealed, wholly existential; he is just what he is, freed from paranoid concealment, from the knowledge of his secrets and his secret knowledge."[5]

This brings me to another particular person who made an impression on my life. Hugh Bishop, like Herbert Kelly, was an Anglican monk. He shared the gift of transparency in that he had the skill of seeing and seeing through others. He was the warden (the dean) of the seminary where I was a student and eventually became superior of the religious order of which he was a member. He shocked the religious world in England by doubting his faith publicly on national television and by leaving the community to live with a younger man. Hugh died full of years and very happy, a faithful minister of the gospel. He made mistakes. He could be difficult and insufferable, but he was a romantic, a lover. He taught me more than anyone about what it means to be ordained. He wasn't a role model in the traditional sense. I have no desire to be like him or to do what he did, but I do hope that I can be as true to myself as he was to himself. There was something in him one could trust. And that, in the end, is what I want. What or who, in the end, can I trust? How far can I trust the bits and pieces of the story of how my faith came to be the way it is? How do I sort out the truth about me and my ministry from its cultural shaping, from the accidents of history?

Our Christianity is inevitably polluted (at worst) and grounded (at best) by a particular time and place. That's why I believe that my life has been graced by particular people, by Herbert Kelly and Hugh Bishop and a host of others. What have they done? They have, formally and informally, been my spiritual guides. They have graciously introduced me to a new story for myself. They have taught me that every character in that inner theater of the self has a part to play. They have also shown up the distortions in my version of my story and have saved me from myself. They not only showed me the way the universe is ordered but revealed to me the way that those of us who happen to be ordained can share in God's ordering of the world.

Moving Through Lies and
Half-Truths into Community

The way I understand my first twenty-four years growing up in England is to realize they were full of lies and half-truths. It's like seeing myself in the broken fragments of a distorting mirror. I need the perspective of others who love me to show me a truer picture. My spiritual guides have looked right through me and have been instruments of healing and forgiveness. I have been looked at lovingly in silence and have been healed. Clergy who do just that are often, for me, the best evangelists. Such a contemplative attitude is all too rare in the age of "poor, little, talkative Christianity." Many clergy know little about silence and contemplation. We only know how to talk.

I stop for breath. God is One. I am legion. I take a look at myself and I find that I am multiform in my believing: English and American; Protestant and Catholic; orthodox yet willing to listen to the needs and insights behind the New Age movement; Anglo-Catholic and Evangelical —inconsistent yet with continuity. I am a walking miracle of grace in an ecumenical zoo. I am not *one* thing. I have found congruency with Plymouth Brethren, Baptist ministers, and Tibetan monks. I have my prejudices, and I am always looking for a theological fight. Yet I also ache for the time when the tribe (which includes my own psychic zoo) gathers around the altar "fire" to share stories and to break bread.

Novelist Margaret Drabble describes accurately my experience of myself in the company of others (an experience I call "Church"): "We are all part of a whole which has its own, its distinct, its other meaning; we are not ourselves, we are crossroads, meeting places, points on a curve, we cannot exist independently for we are nothing but signs, conjunctions, aggregations."[6]

What I find is the constant reconstruction of the horizon of my expectations, the unnerving formation and alteration of my perceptions. What is constant? What is changing? I cling to the illusion of fixed phrases and forms. I am blind to my endless experimentation with values. What abides in the conflict of interpretation?

In the middle of all this chaotic relativism is there universal significance? Yes, there is, and it is mediated through persons, who know that we belong to one another. Christianity is about incarnation, and the truth of God is revealed in and through our being members one of another. I need reminders of the mystery, hesitation, and hiddenness of my experience, especially religious experience. My reminders are the Hugh Bishops and Herbert Kellys of this world, actual people, as arrogant and as compromised as they are sometimes. My reminders are my fellow ministers who even in their failure feed me and heal me.

The World Still Needs Lovers

What has it been like to be a priest in the middle of all this? I have been one for twenty-five years, and I have experienced a great many changes, internally in my own spiritual life and externally in the institutional Church.

Love is a work of the passionate imagination. It has intellectual bite as well as emotional impact. Hugh Bishop taught me that to be a priest simply means to be in love. I realize "love" language makes certain people in the Church nervous not only because of our fear of the erotic (which we continue to confuse with the narrowly sexual) but also with its inevitably leading us into the unknown and untried. But we do have a need for people to take the risk of deep friendship. The Church needs lovers. The Church needs those who know the secret of self-offering, the secret of sacrifice and delight.

CHAPTER TWO

Daring to Be Ordained

When someone comes to me for advice about ordination I always suggest that he or she avoid it if at all possible! Ordination should be a last resort, the final response to a lover who will not let go. There must be the elements of romance and delight.

I refer them to the story in the Old Testament of Jacob's encounter with the angel of God (Gen. 32:22) with its fourfold pattern of struggle, wounding, naming, and blessing. Jacob is given a new name (a new identity) and God's blessing only after being wounded. This is a pattern for every human being who is open to the Spirit, but one that is particularly appropriate for those who think that they might have a vocation to the ordained ministry.

One of the saddest things I have had to do is counsel those who have drifted into ordination in a haze of idealism. They failed to count the cost. Ordination is not a pathway to self-fulfillment, still less the prescribed way to be a real Christian. Avoid it if you can. And if you can't avoid it, say "Yes!" to it with a clear eye and open heart. It should be embraced only as a passion and not undertaken as a meal ticket or a career. I experienced a deep sense of freedom when I realized that I still wanted to be a priest even if I couldn't earn my living that way.

Some clergy are literally trapped in their ministry. They think that there is no way out. Somewhere along the way they lost or mislaid their humanity. They have grown to dread the ministry, even to hate it, and the various denominations need to develop strategies and set aside finances to help men and women leave the ordained ministry without shame or bitterness. To be ordained is first to be truly human.

There Is No Pure Motive

We decide to be ordained for a variety of motives largely hidden from us at the time. My motives for seeking ordination were a mixture of two desires. One was for upward mobility (anything to get off what seemed to be my family's unambitious, depressingly fatalistic treadmill). Embedded in my call to priesthood was a fear of weakness and power-lessness. Little did I know that I was embracing the very things I dreaded. Later on (more than twenty years later) it was a fear I had to confront. The second desire was to save the world—single-handedly!

With regard to the former, I saw the Church of England as unrepen-tantly elitist in the way it selected men for ordination, and I wanted to get in with the powerful people. As it happens, I was mistaken. By the time I was ordained, and certainly by the time I came to teach in an English theological college, bishops were ordaining quite common folk, even riffraff! The bishops still belonged to the old-boy network, but the general run-of-the-mill clergy were ordinary people just like me. Such was the myth that had me in its thrall. I felt rather like Groucho Marx— I didn't want to belong to a club that would accept the likes of me as a member.

With regard to my desire to save the world, I had attended a fiercely evangelical Sunday school and felt I knew what was needed to save the world. It all sounds naive now, but I believe somehow God was in my desire too.

Being Human and Being Different

My two grandmothers symbolized the conflict that was to come. My father's mother was one of those naturally good people. She wasn't good in a cloying way. She was simply guileless. She was *pious* in the best sense of the word. She encouraged me in my first gropings toward priesthood and was always loving and supportive. She died when I was a teenager. Recently I came across her one and only letter to me telling me how much she admired me and to persevere with my vocation. At the time, no doubt, this puffed me up, but it was special to be admired by the wisest woman I knew. She understood that the clergy are "different."

My mother's mother, on the other hand, was far from pious. She was a canny, crafty, and resourceful country woman who bore thirteen children and wasn't above a little "flutter" (a bet) on the horses. She was slippery, but she was alive! She took delight in things. When she heard that I was seeking ordination ("going into the Church" it was called), she exclaimed, "I hope to Christ he's not!" This was not a pious utterance! She was very grounded, very human. She thought the clergy were of "no earthly use."

My two delightful grandmothers symbolize the two important characteristics for me with regard to the priesthood: one is the need freely to embrace difference, the need for vision, springing from the life of prayer; the other is the need to be grounded, to be "earthed," to be human.

I treasure the examples of both grandmothers and I wouldn't want to judge one as closer to God than the other. Their contributions to my sense of vocation can be summed up in the command to be "wise as serpents and harmless as doves." I am now in the process of beginning to reclaim the heritage of my two grandmothers—an earthed faith and faithfulness that does not ask me to be superhuman. In their different ways, they knew God's delight.

The Humanly Human Path to Ordination

My vocation to the ordained ministry began when I was at a youth weekend. I must have made myself a nuisance, because I remember the chaplain barking at me after I had disrupted a discussion about the church by lampooning the clergy. "If you're so good," he snapped, "why don't you volunteer and come on in and do better." His rebuke shut me up and stuck in my throat for years. Meanwhile I had left the safety of militant evangelicalism (although it made a deeper impression on me than I realized) and was flirting with "the Truth" of Roman Catholicism. I still had my zippered Bible with the inscription in the flyleaf: "Alan Jones—a slave of Christ." I must have been an insufferable prig. I was also a confused and driven working-class boy desperately trying to "rise above my station." I was also, thank God and in spite of myself, wanting to be "a slave of Christ." I became a missionary candidate for the Society for the Propagation of the Gospel and didn't relinquish (or fulfill—it depends on your point of view) my candidacy until I emigrated to the United States in 1964. In all the confusion and the mess that was and is Alan Jones, I can now discern the mercy and delight of God.

"For Their Sakes I Consecrate Myself"

I'm glad that I'm ordained, but I had no real idea what I was getting into twenty-five years ago. Is it perhaps best that we don't entirely know what we're doing at the key turning points in our lives? No one who is wide awake would dare to be ordained. It is part of the mercy of God that we can see only a few steps ahead of us. Twenty-five years ago I was driven by a wild desire to "do" something with my life. Ordination was a great romance, and I rushed into it blindly.

I remember a meditation on the priesthood Hugh Bishop gave in the chapel of the College of the Resurrection in Yorkshire in 1963. It was on the text "For *their* sakes I consecrate myself" (John 17:19). These are the words of Jesus as he prepares himself for his Passion. They had and still have a profound effect on me. Over twenty-five years ago they struck me (a very idealistic and naive twenty-three-year-old) with tremendous force. It may seem outrageous for us young men, all those years ago, to have taken the words of Jesus' great prayer as our own, but we did. I do. I don't do it consistently or very well, but I do.

I was taught that at the center of priesthood is self-offering. The self-understanding of the priest is shaped by the knowledge that every human being is given a "priestly" identity. To be a priest is to know what it is to be blessed and to bless in return. The fully human life is a consecrated life in the service of others. An ordained minister (like every human being) needs to be someone who is in touch with the delight and joy at the heart of things that allows the service to be truly free and not drudgery.

My own unhappiness with being ordained has tended to be merely a reflection of my own unhappiness with myself. My issues are spiritual and psychological, internal rather than external.

This is not to say that there aren't external problems with the institutional Church. In my more jaundiced moments all I can see are its petty politics, its lack of nerve, its general and pathetic veniality. Then there are the Church leaders (in my tradition, bishops) who, at least in the United States, tend to see themselves merely as managers; some are liberal de-mythologizers who with secularizing zeal assault the old and naive certainties of their flocks. Others remain stiff and ignorant "traditionalists."

But I cannot maintain a jaundiced view for long, not least because such a view is a distortion, and maintaining a twisted vision is a terrible strain. Bishop-bashing and blaming our leaders have always been cheap and easy but in the end are unsatisfying. Lies and half-truths take a great deal of time and effort to keep up. This is as true for institutions as it is for individuals. These half-truths are not the issue anyway. The issue is far deeper and has to do with our self-understanding as persons, with our sense of identity in God. It has to do with Catholicity—wholeness in all its senses—personal and communal, intellectual and emotional, private and political.

Powerlessness, Ignorance, and Dispossession

Those who are ordained should know firsthand about the peculiar spiritual gifts that are given us when we understand ourselves to be defined by boundless mystery and a limitless horizon. When we know we stand before uncontrollable mystery, we will realize just how puny our power, wisdom, and possessions really are. To stand in the presence of God is to experience powerlessness, ignorance, and dispossession. This would be terrifying if it were not for the fact that the One before whom we stand is the God of love. To stand in that presence is liberating.

Ministers are God-symbols, whether we know it or not, whether we like it or not. The divine gifts of powerlessness, ignorance, and dispossession are part of the Christian's arsenal and are given especially to the clergy, so that we don't go mad either with inflation, thinking we are God, or with depression, thinking that we or someone has made a terrible mistake in giving us this task in the first place. Such gifts bring us up from ruin to restoration. A genuine sense of ministry is often born out of a feeling of failure and an experience of ruin. I don't mean that there has to be some public scandal or that the failure and ruin have to be visible. I am speaking more of an inner experience of spiritual bankruptcy that lays the groundwork for the deeper experience of grace.

All Christians are invited to learn one of the powerful lessons of the gospel that the privileged access to the grace of God is through our being in touch with our greatest weakness. Millions have and are recovering their sanity and proper self-love through the various twelve-step programs originating with Alcoholics Anonymous. They know that the road back is through the narrow door of powerlessness. Those who know this are true ministers of the gospel.

Great spiritual directors know firsthand of the divine power available to us once we have come face to face with our own powerlessness. Monica Furlong, in her biography of Alan Watts (an errant Anglican priest), shows us the mirror image of a person unable to face his own terrible, aching need. For someone like Watts to accept spiritual help was terrifying because it pushed him back into being dependent on someone. "There was in him a mixture of longing and fear, of self-destructive willfulness and calculated self-interest, which made it too difficult to accept help. . . . To refuse so much wisdom and loving care, however skillfully he rationalized it, reduced him to isolation, which, for all his marvelous openness, produced a kind of rigidity, the rigidity that comes from self-sufficiency, from always 'knowing better.'"[1]

Many ministers have neither the inner resources nor the means of asking for help with regard to their passions and longings. We do not know how to tell the truth about ourselves and our world. And if we clergy feel untouched by any of these problems, we might ask ourselves, How much wildness and passion is there in us? How far have we fallen away from our first love? Being able to seek and ask for help frees us to dare to be ordained.

We become priests and ministers for a variety of motives, motives largely hidden from us at the time. One of the monks of Father Kelly's community (the Society of the Sacred Mission) told me, "My son, never examine your motives. They're bound to be vile and disgusting!" How did I dare offer myself for ordination? I was nineteen and didn't know better. But it wasn't my "knowing" anything that led me into ordination. I believe it was the Holy Spirit working through my muddle.

Being Human—Being Different

Why are people surprised when they discover that clergy are human? Why do they make a thing of it? A local newspaper that still has a religion page published an article titled, "Gosh darn it! Believe it or not ministers swear, too. Ministers of the cloth try not to cuss." It was a lighthearted piece of frothy journalism but symptomatic of one of the irritants of being a minister. It is annoying after a while to have one's humanity made into a minor revelation! On the other hand, being thought of as different from others goes with the territory of ministry. We are human.

We are different, set apart. That's the way it is. But if we aren't rooted in our humanity, being ordained will poison and destroy us.

What does it feel like to be a public figure? It is hard to describe because of the tension between our ordinariness as human beings and our calling as pastors. From the outside, priests or ministers, seen through the prism of others' hopes and prejudices, serve quite rightly symbolic functions for the community. They can be figures of fun, persons to be feared, or persons who will be there when disaster strikes. The point of view will depend on the culture in which ministers live. Ministers are screens onto which are projected people's hang-ups and their legitimate expectations. I find it as hard to be adored (for no reason other than my role) as to be judged a fool just because I'm a minister. Such projections, however, go with the territory. They are part of the job description of the pastor.

People have their own views, from the wildly positive to the bitterly negative. My grandmother was convinced that all doctors and parsons were rogues! They had to be. Who could possibly live up to the ideals of such professions? Others almost drool with admiration in the presence of a minister or a doctor. The clergy I know have feelings about their vocation that reflect these extreme positions. There are the arrogant who develop a thick-skinned infallibility about their gifts and powers. Others are racked with guilt and self-doubt, tormented with questions: "Should I be doing this? Maybe I should quit?"

I have tended to swing on a pendulum between an unjustified self-confidence to self-pitying thoughts of unworthiness. Both extremes are seductive in that they concentrate our attention on the self and its concerns. It takes a robust personality to cope with the projections of others, who see priests as either saints or hypocrites. Then there are the inner uncertainties of the individual minister's soul. I see my own ups and downs, my failures and moments of faithfulness as an Episcopal priest, as an expression of my determination to be as humanly human as possible. I am committed to doing this without denying the role I have been called to fulfill in the important games communities need to play to learn compassion and stay human.

The Wounds and Weaknesses of Ministers

All the ministers who have influenced me have struggled with wounds and weaknesses. Some drank too much ("the whisky priests").

For others sexuality was an abiding wound. There were the lazy, the prophetic, and the neurotic. There were also the doggedly loyal ones who nevertheless ran afoul of the system. All in all there has been pain and waste. Some were scholars, others were unreflective activists. Some were family men, others homosexuals, those who denied it and those who came to terms with it by learning to love themselves as God made them. There were the genuine celibates, who had found a way not to suppress their sexuality but to channel it. There are now the women who have demonstrated that their ordination moves us closer to that Catholicity for which the world longs. There are my priest friends living with AIDS, each of them an inspiration. All have touched me deeply and I am grateful to them for being humanly human. They have taught me that God is always trying to reach me and that God is continually giving himself to me.

The so-called failed ones who touch me most are those who struggled to be *in* their bodies, real and enfleshed human beings, with temptations, appetites, and longings that were large and demanding. I think of a good friend who recently came to the end of his rope. He had just been elected a bishop, the pinnacle of all that he thought he desired. Much to his amazement, he declined the position and went into a terrible depression. One afternoon, not long before Christmas, he entered the abyss. He stole twelve pairs of white socks from a department store, tried to buy a revolver to kill himself, and finally was caught being propositioned by a male prostitute in a public lavatory. The press had a high time. His bishop gave him wonderful support, as did his wife and family. He sought and received spiritual and psychological help, and he is now on the road to recovery. He knows what it is to be healed and forgiven. He is a free man.

I'm not suggesting that true priesthood resides in our falling apart, going crazy, or becoming self-indulgent. I simply insist that whatever kind of minister we are called to be, our vocation must take into account our full humanity, its longings and its passions.

By the time I came to be ordained in 1966, I tried to leave the romance and longings behind. I denied the hunger. My evangelical training gave me no help understanding my longings, least of all the erotic ones. Over the years, my longings had to be honored and retrieved. I thought, "If they really knew what I was like, they'd never allow me to be ordained." I felt this fear at my ordination, an Anglo-Catholic liturgical opera, at St. Peter's Streatham in London, badly played and under-rehearsed. I didn't so much think that I was making a mistake as that the bishop was. He seemed a vain and distant man, very full of himself. I was swept along by events and deeply moved in spite of the emptiness of the ceremonial.

But I took with me from my ordination the wounding burden of my secret self, with the enormity of what I had dared. I was burdened with an unfamiliar and cumbersome persona and had neither the skill nor the wisdom to wear it for the love of God. I also took with me my desire for security and power. This desire was killing me spiritually and had to be confronted and redirected. I had to learn the true nature of power per-fected in weakness.

The truly Christian ministry requires the ordinary stuff of friendship and love. Priests need them for their own sake even more than for the sake of others. If they aren't warmed by them, the minister becomes "a naked animal raging with the cold and with his own released wildness."[2] Blood must be allowed to flow through our veins.

All of us have our peculiarities and particularities, our vulnerabil-ities, impairments, and disabilities. The wisest among us know that friendship, spiritual direction, prayer, relaxation, the ability to have fun and to give ourselves to others save us from being suffocated and over-come by a sense of failure, from being seduced by the voice inside that tells us we are no good. We are forced to ask terrifying questions. Will I make it? Will I fail? Will I be abandoned? How will I visit the sick? How will I sit with the dying?

The Word of Forgiveness and
the Naming of a Lie

For me ministry seen from the inside is nowhere better expressed than by the American novelist Frederick Buechner. Let me cite just two examples: his story about how one minister learned the mystery of his calling, and his account of his father's suicide.

In the novel *The Final Beast,* Rooney, troubled by an act of adultery in her past, has run away. Her pastor goes after her and finds her in the home of her friend Lillian, who speaks to him while Rooney is upstairs.

"Oh Lord, how advice bores me, especially when it's good. And yours was good enough. 'Go back to your husband.' That probably didn't come so easy, did it? 'Forget your infidelity.' . . . It's so modern, and it's so sane, and it's just the advice she'd want if she wanted advice. Only give her what she really wants . . . "

"Give her what, for Christ's sake?"

"For Christ's sake . . . The only thing you have to give." And then she almost shouted at him. "Forgive her for Christ's sake, little priest!"

"But she knows I forgive her."

"She doesn't know God forgives her. That's the only power you have —to tell her that. Not just that he forgives the poor little adultery. But the faces she can't bear to look at now. The man's. Her husband's. Her own, half the time. Tell her God forgives her for being lonely and bored, for not being full of joy with a house full of children. That's what sin really is, you know—not being full of joy. Tell her that sin is forgiven whether she knows it or not, that's what she wants more than anything else—what all of us want. What on earth do you think you were ordained for?"[3]

I can't think of anything more glorious for a priest to do than to declare, "Go in peace. The Lord has put away all your sins. And pray for me, a sinner." I cannot think of anything more terrible than not to know its joy.

Buechner's father's suicide is a deeply sad commentary on a man who was incapable of forgiving himself. "It was not for several days that a note was found. It was written in pencil on the last page of *Gone with the Wind,* which had been published that year, 1936, and it was addressed to my mother. 'I adore you and love you,' it said, 'and I am no good. . . . Give Freddie my watch. Give Jamie my pearl pin. I give you all my love.'"[4] The minister is there to name that last phrase, "I am no good," as a lie. It is a deep and cruel lie tormenting and ruining many a human being.

The Ministers of the Future

Tomorrow's priests will be (otherwise they will not exist at all) persons able to listen, to whom all individuals matter even though they are of no social or political importance; persons in whom one can confide, who practice the holy folly, or try to, of bearing not only their own

22

burdens but also those of others because they know the mystery of sub-stitution. The priests of tomorrow will not join in the neurotic pursuit of wealth and security but will refuse the painkillers for the dreadful dis-appointment of existence. They cannot be ecclesiastical civil servants but will be persons who because of inner experience believe, hope, and love.[5]

My experience of the ordained priesthood—God's peculiar way of saving my soul—has been one of deep failure with regard to my discov-ering a credible Catholicism. I have come to believe that Catholicism or Protestantism-as-ideology is, in fact, a seductive and damaging addic-tion. I am continually "surprised by grace," by being formed by particular souls who teach me that the gospel is both a given and gift.

The French priest Jean Sulivan wrote:

> But can we expect all university professors to be pioneers, all parish priests to be prophets, all bishops to be successors of the apostles? Each of them has been recruited haphazardly, with his own share of good will, insight and blindness, his own wounds and ambitions. I'm not shocked by this. I'm not preaching purity. Jesus is delivered up; he always will be. . . . What is . . . amazing is that always, within the womb of illusion and hypocrisy, lost in the crowd, there have been saints. The word has never ceased finding its way into the flesh of men and women. Our task is to live the benediction and the insurrection at the same time, the love and the humor, the unimportance of everything and its infinite importance.[6]

In that context we dare to consecrate ourselves for others. Only with the knowledge that one is loved does the true daring of self-offering come.

What Happens When
We Say "Yes!" to the Call?

Ordination is one way a disciple of Jesus Christ loses her or his life to find it. My love of the priesthood has been lost and recovered over and over again. For me it has been a case of falling away and finding myself returning to the good news of the gospel in a deeper way. I find that the Easter story of death and new life is true, not just "out there" but inside me. My priesthood is me, not in the outward trappings. I sense in myself the beginnings of a grace-filled resolution of the tension between being "human" and being "different." Being a minister (good, bad, and indifferent) is who I am. Ordination has been for me the instrument by which I have grown into the man that I am. Through it I have become acquainted with the birthright of everyone who comes into being as a gift of God. Through it I have come to a sense of myself as God's child, unique and unrepeatable.

Ordination gave me a voice to tell the love story of the gospel not because the story belongs to me but because it belongs to everyone. Clergy are "different" only in the sense that they are signs, like audiovisual aids, of what all people essentially are, children of God and therefore brothers and sisters to everyone.

Being Oneself and Playing a Role

Some of the most famous "lyrics" describing the ordained priest are found in Chaucer's *Canterbury Tales*:

> Wide was his parish, with houses far asunder
> Yet he neglected not in rain or thunder,
> In sickness or in grief to pay a call
> On the remotest whether great or small
> Upon his feet, and in his hand a stave.
> This noble example to his sheep he gave,
> First following the word before he taught it,
> And it was from the gospel he had caught it.
> This little proverb he would add thereto
> That if gold rust what then will iron do?
> For if a priest be foul in whom we trust
> No wonder that a common man should rust;
> And shame it is to see—let priests take stock—
> A shitten shepherd and a snowy flock.[7]

This passage sums up the call of ministers in pastoral terms. The first few lines say something about their duties, the rest speak to the manner of life. There is truth to the notion that the life of faith is best caught rather than taught. The last four lines state clearly the tension between the call to be human and the call to be different. It is legitimate that the ordained be judged by a higher standard than their flocks because we rightly expect spiritual leaders to lead.

André Malraux wrote, "All vocations arouse hatred." My maternal grandmother would have approved. Immoral judges, doctors, and lawyers (insofar as these are still vocations) are somehow worse than immoral plumbers and bus drivers, because they deal with our souls, with our inner selves. They mess with who we are. "The swindler does not provoke the same feelings as does the cowardly officer, the simoniac priest or the corrupt judge, because these men are in uniform, when they are false to their vocations, become usurpers."[8] I think this may be an unnecessary elitist distinction. The real difference has something to do with role and visibility. The more one is in the limelight playing a certain and important role for society, the more likely one is to get hit. Priests are sitting targets in ways waiters are not. Building and plumbing can be vocations as well as priesthood and medicine. Nevertheless Malraux's point is worth considering: "All vocations arouse hatred." And if not hatred, then outrage and disappointment.

With Romance, Disappointment Is Built In

Christianity is a romance and Christians are above all romantics. There will always be a sense of disappointment. We are never quite the lovers we would like to be. As we have seen, the role of the ordained in this love affair is very peculiar in that we have to be in two places at once. We are called to be both members of the people of God (human) and yet servants, even teachers of love, within the Body of Christ. I find it enormously hard to fulfill my vocation as a priest. Not only am I a poor lover, I often lack the will to learn. Yet I wouldn't trade the struggle for anything else in the world, and that in spite of my weaknesses and the general superficiality of much religion.

I take great comfort from the advice Cardinal Mercier was said to have given his ordinands on the night before their ordination: "Gentlemen, remember God has called you to be priests because he cannot trust you to be laymen!" This is another way of saying Saint Augustine's famous phrase, "What I am for you appalls me. What I am with you consoles me. For you I am a bishop, with you I am a Christian." This is an accurate summation of the tension in the ordained ministry and the way it is endured and enjoyed.

My success or failure does nothing to invalidate the faithfulness of the One who made us and loves us. One thing that keeps me traveling hopefully as a public servant of Christ has to do with the weight I give my failure. I take my sins seriously, but none of them outweighs the love at the heart of things. None of them invalidates the Way I am following.

Leo Tolstoy serves as an inspiration in this regard. He had great failings, but he has deepened humanity's soul. The novelist A. N. Wilson was "haunted by [Tolstoy's] appalling domestic sufferings." In many ways Tolstoy was a pathetic figure with foolish prejudices and large appetites. He was a moral failure. Just as he had resolved to put all anger out of his heart, he would lose his temper. "Nor was it necessarily safe for the young peasant girls to get too close to the Count after he made his notorious vow of complete celibacy." Tolstoy had an answer to shame his detractors that I find comforting. He was haunted by the obvious fact that he could not practice what he preached. Everyone knew it. He made outrageous gospel claims with regard to human conduct and fell flat on his face over and over again. He wished he could preach by deeds.

> I do not fulfil a ten-thousandth part [of the Christian commandments] it is true, and I am to blame for that; but it is not because I do not wish to fulfil them that I fail, but because I do not know how to. Teach me how to escape the nets of temptation that have ensnared me, help me, and I will fulfil them; but even without help I desire and hope to do so. Blame me— I do that myself—but blame *me,* and not the path I tread. . . . If I know the road home and go along it drunk, staggering from side to side—does that make the road along which I go the wrong one?[9]

I believe I am on the right path and that path can be trusted, but I sometimes stagger along it. I am not always attentive, but someone or something always draws me on. On occasions I see something of the One whose love holds all things in being.

Do I sound romantic? I am. And why not? How else will the gift of love circulate among us? I know that I am blessed, and I want to bless in return. I know that the ground in which my ministry flourishes is my humanity—warts and all. I also know that we are deepened by simple human interaction: we come to new birth through the agency of one another's ministry.

In the End, Only Christ

George Tyrrell, an Irish Jesuit who died at the beginning of this century and was shamefully excommunicated as a "modernist," wrote a meditation on the solemn celebration of Tenebrae in Holy Week. A seven-branched candelabra is placed on the altar, and this is the only illumination in the church. As the choir sings the powerful verses from Scripture, the candles are extinguished one at a time, until only the central one is left. Father Tyrrell suggests that this is a sign of the Christian pilgrimage. Slowly all the old supports are taken away—our reliance on our education, our class, our skill—and all that is left is one solitary light, the light of Christ. We are brought to the end of our rope. We have nothing left to negotiate with. We are naked, exposed, and human before God.

This secret I too received at my ordination, the secret that God uses frail human instruments to fulfill the divine purpose. Something deeper than I had ever dreamed had gone on in that sacrament in St. Peter's Church, Streatham, on 29 June 1966.

> *Thou art a priest forever, forever, forever.* Deeper than wounds that slit flesh, muscle and ligament to the bone, deeper than fracture of the poor bony frame, deeper than the most intense experience such as could, on merely being recalled, start the heart racing and the little glands secreting the juice of fear or passion, deeper than those went the print of the sacrament. *Thou art a priest.*[10]

I have come to believe that my ordination was the wound of delight. I often forget it, but I am indelibly marked by it. I am grateful.

CHAPTER THREE

The Minister—
God's Wounded Fool

W hat comes to mind when we use the image of the wounded healer? The danger is to pay more attention to the wounding than to the healing. God's loving us comes as a kind of wounding, but it is the kind of wounding that heals, just as the powerlessness we encounter turns out to be true power. In "The Living Flame of Love," Saint John of the Cross wrote of the God who wounded him to cure him: "You touched me with the touch of the splendor of your glory . . . you touched me with the force of your cautery (the Holy Spirit—the Living Flame) and wounded me."[1] Love as a kind of wound is well attested to in poetry addressed either to God or to a human lover. It cannot be apprehended except through the symbolism of sacrifice and substitution.

In the mystery of love our wounds are not only healed but are "exchanged" in the act of substitution. Under the mercy of God, we can experience the woundedness of others and be bearers of healing to each other. For example, I know of someone who was facing a serious operation. She couldn't sleep at night because she was worried and anxious. A friend offered to "take on" her worry and anxiety, through the ministry of intercession. The woman could rest and was able to face her operation with faith and confidence.

We can, for a while, take on the woundedness of others. How? When it comes to matters of the Spirit, we share in an amazing network of solidarity with others. Sometimes it is not a matter of conscious choice. For some reason or another, the drama of another person's life is lived through us, even without our consent. The unresolved drama in a parent's life is often played out by the child. Part of the work of the Spirit is to make us aware of these dramas and to resolve them by choosing freely to live through them. I know others have suffered for me and have endured things on my behalf. Responding to the call to be God's wounded fool gives us an opportunity to help others through the drama of their lives.

The Solidarity of Substitution

In our age of extreme individualism, the idea of substitution is very difficult for us to understand or accept. During the terror of the French Revolution, the religious orders were suppressed. Their members were dispersed, and if they resisted, they were sent to the guillotine. Francis Poulenc's beautiful opera *Dialogues of the Carmelites* is set in this period. Blanche, a neurotic young woman from an aristocratic family, enters the convent just before the Revolution. She is impressed by the calm, rocklike faith of the mother superior. When the old nun is on her deathbed, her firm faith appears to desert her, and, much to the surprise and dismay of the sisters, she dies in darkness and terror. The rage of the Revolution soon reaches the convent, and the sisters are forced to go their separate ways. Blanche flees, but some of the sisters refuse to leave and are sent to the guillotine.

Blanche hides herself in the crowd that has gathered to watch the executions. The sisters go to their death singing the *Salve Regina*. The execution is offstage, and as they leave to die, the voices singing the hymn are fewer and fewer. When the last sister has gone, Blanche emerges from the crowd singing the *Salve Regina* in a strong clear voice. This formerly neurotic girl is now a woman of rocklike faith. She faces death with love and courage. The suggestion is that there had been a substitution, an exchange. The mother superior had taken on Blanche's terror and had died her death for her. Blanche was able, through the mystery of substitution, to die well in the face of persecution.

Life is full of such substitutions—on a smaller scale of course, but nonetheless real. I know that people have endured suffering and pain for my sake. The notions of sacrifice and substitution can be understood only within the context of romantic love.

Love and Neurosis

The priest is a sign of the longing of love, and that longing can easily degenerate into neurosis. "Wounded healers" can get into trouble. Thomas Maeder makes much of the fact that "the 'helping professions,' notably psychotherapy and the ministry, appear to attract more than their share of the emotionally unstable."[2] I suppose the Church should be the haven of the emotionally disturbed and the spiritually shipwrecked. Perhaps we should not be surprised at clerical pathology. What should surprise and even outrage us is our unwillingness to name it and face it as a people. There seems to be a gospel—good news—for everyone except the clergy. According to Maeder, psychological studies of the ordained "suggest a high incidence of family problems and narcissistic disorders, and a host of other problems involving interpersonal relations and self-esteem."

I know that I conform in at least one respect to the type. Like many "healers," I was virtually an only child (my brother and sister were much older than I). My father died when I was twelve. My parents were "inadequate" (there is no greater sign of incompetence than a parent's dying!). After my father died, my mother seemed to live her life in a perpetual low-grade depression. It did lift occasionally, when a grandchild was born or a happy memory came unbidden to her mind, but for the most part she was trapped in an unreliable and hostile world. I was obliged to become a "little adult."

Evidently this is a characteristic of many "healers." The child is "rushed through childhood too quickly, without the warmth, the protection, and the love that children deserve. . . . Such people grow up believing that hard work and responsibility are the only things that give them value in other's eyes."[3] Certainly there are clergy who are on a treadmill of their selfishly selfless labors. Maeder quotes an unidentified Jungian analyst who is also an Episcopal priest: "These people are pathological givers. . . . They have given so much that they finally run out of spiritual and nervous energy, and what remains is the underlying resentment. You find a great deal of resentment and sourness among the clergy."

31

How do ministers cope with their resentment? There are, evidently, two types of clergy—the repentant sinner and the sealed-off and soured sinner. The former is able to work through her resentment by identifying with other weak and fragile human beings and engage with them in a shared pilgrimage. For the latter, resentment is a useful mask to hide his deep sense of failure and disappointment. An extreme form of the sealed-off sinner "is the rigid and damning preacher. . . . These preachers are so deeply beset by uncertainty and unresolved problems that they have organized their external life through sheer brute force and imposture, but they have left their internal life untouched."[4]

The Fool Who Knows How to Receive

Then there are clergy with authority problems, who want to be accountable only to "God" and who are unable to distinguish their own neurotic and even pathological agenda from the imperatives of the gospel. It all comes down to the minister's inability to receive. Some years ago I was led through a meditation technique that shocked me into recognizing my own pathology in this regard. I was invited to walk in my imagination through a sunlit wood. The path eventually opened up into a beautiful meadow at the edge of which was a little cottage or hut. I went up to the door and opened it. I was told that inside I would meet my teacher and guide, someone who loved me and cared for me. I was instructed to sit for a while and enjoy my teacher's company. After a while I was to formulate a question in my mind and ask my guide for an answer.

My teacher was waiting for me when I opened the door. He was an old man but not frail, someone with immense authority. He looked like a cross between Archbishop Anthony Bloom and William Blake's "Ancient of Days." I sat in his company for a while and we were surrounded and connected by light. A question formed itself in my mind and I spoke: "How can I be a more healing presence?" Even in my meditative state, I was pleased with my "profound" question and with myself. To my surprise my teacher turned angrily toward me. His eyes flashed in fury. "Alan, why do you always ask the wrong questions? You will never become a truly healing presence until you learn to accept healing from others!"

32

This visionary meditation was a turning point in my life. I began a long and ongoing process of learning what it might mean to receive as well as give.

One image of the priest that has always appealed to me is that of the "fool" or "joker." Simon Darcourt, the Anglican priest "hero" in Robertson Davies's *Lyre of Orpheus*, sees himself as the figure of the Fool/Priest in the tarot cards: "The Fool; the cheerful rogue on the journey, with a rip in his pants, and little dog that nipped at his exposed rump, urging him onward and sometimes nudging him in directions he had never intended to take. The Fool, who had no number but the potent zero which, when it was added to any other number, multiplied its significance by ten . . . "[5]

What a metaphor for the ordained ministry—to play the role of the zero! The great round O, the pregnant "Nothing" is the sign of total trust. It is the sign of powerlessness and ignorance in the world's terms. It raises terrifying questions. Will I make it? Will I fail? Will I be abandoned? Sometimes the minister is truly a zero, and all he has to give is his emptiness. All that shows is his weakness. At such moments, he does not play the role of fool. He is one. Roles are sometimes peeled away, and all that remains is the naked self.

The role of the minister is sometimes to have no role, like the joker in a pack of cards. We often play a family game called Spite and Malice. It is for two players and uses two packs of cards. The four jokers are wild cards and can play any role the game demands. The minister is called to be so clear with regard to his identity that he can play the role of the two or the king or queen, depending on the requirements of the game. Are you free enough to play the role that life demands of you at this particular moment? Is your rejection of the fact that you are blessed and are to bless in return an escape from the role of the fool or joker? Are you one of those people who "do not go into the forests to seek what they are, but to forget what they suspect themselves to be"?[6]

In screening candidates for the ordained ministry, a bishop asks himself, "Is this a whole person seeking to express his wholeness through the ministry? Or is this a person trying to *find* his wholeness in the ministry?" I can see what the bishop is driving at, but I would want to put the question in terms of self-knowledge and the ability to cope rather than in terms of wholeness. I would be very suspicious of a man or woman who claimed to enjoy a wholeness that was ready to be expressed in ministry. "There should be no doubt that the healer, too, is wounded. But his gift, his ministry, is not in exhibiting his wounds, but in leading others to the source of healing where he, despite himself, is healed."[7] This is true, but I am not quite ready to abandon the metaphor of the wounded healer altogether, although there are signs that it (used by Henri Nouwen over twenty years ago) may be in need of reinterpretation. Its application to the ordained ministry has been misused if not abused. Has the ministry become all wound and no healing? Perhaps some of us have milked the metaphor dry? Dennis Campbell, dean of the Divinity School at Duke University, "wondered if the image had not outlived its usefulness. Seminarians and clergy, he suggested, had become practiced at grabbing hold of the adjective to justify the incessant exhibition of their wounds. Stewing in their discontents, clergy are increasingly given to whining and self-pity. Preoccupation with being 'wounded' blocks attention to their call to be 'healer.'" We have all become thoroughly psychologized—"a near perfect example of the church to what Philip Rieff called 'the therapeutic society.'"[8] To make matters worse, we have largely lost our sense of humor.

Are the Clergy Overpsychologized?

Clergy have an ambivalent attitude to psychology and psychotherapy. Some seem to have allowed their ministry to collapse into the narrowly therapeutic, while others are frightened of anything psychological. Some even believe that psychology is demonic. I have found psychotherapy an invaluable tool in understanding myself and the world I live in, but it is no substitute for the gospel. I have found no direct good news in therapy, but it has often prepared me to receive the good news more deeply.

Robert Coles asks, "Why is it that psychiatry now has so much intellectual, and yes, moral authority among the clergy?" Coles goes on to tell what is for me a hair-raising story about the visit of a priest to a chronically sick man in hospital. One of the things I dread is finding myself terminally ill and being trapped by an eager, young, therapeutically oriented, and humorless clergyman, who will walk all over my psyche by insisting on my sharing my feelings when all I want are the traditional priestly ministrations of prayer and anointing. Robert Coles's sick friend had said to the priest that he was doing "fine," by which he had meant to indicate that he had no great wish to elaborate. The priest simply would not accept that answer and insisted on a line of probing and questioning about the man's psychological state. The priest no doubt meant well, but when the priest left, the patient was feeling annoyed and then became outraged.

> He had wanted to talk with the priest about God and His ways, about Christ's life and death . . . about Heaven and Hell—only to be approached repeatedly with psychological words and phrases. In their entirety those words and phrases constituted a statement, an insinuation: you are in psychological jeopardy, and that is what I, an ordained priest of the Holy Roman Catholic Church, have learned to consider more important than anything else, when in the presence of a person such as you.[9]

The patient was beside himself: "He comes here with a Roman collar, and offers me psychological banalities as God's word!" "The priest was mesmerized by the mind and its commonplace workings—when he was supposed to be a man of The Book, alert to matters *sub specie aeternitatis.*"

Is the patient being unfair, or is he onto something? I think both. There is always the danger of overpsychologizing, but that does not negate the value of psychology in helping us in the godly task of self-knowledge. But the patient was also right to be outraged. Too often the priest has forgotten the marvelous instruments for ministry at his or her disposal. Too often the Bible and its messages are used "as anecdotal adjuncts, quaint leftovers from an earlier era." Too often the priest's "wonderful sacramental responsibilities" are turned into mere habits. Coles concludes, "I wonder whether the deepest mire, the deepest waters, for many of America's clergy, not to mention us laymen, may be found in the dreary solipsistic world so many of us have learned to find interesting: the mind's moods, the various 'stages' and 'phases' of 'human development' or of 'dying,' all dwelt upon (God save us!) as if Stations of the Cross."[10]

More often than not, ministers forget that they are not alone. They stand in a tradition. They are well connected. There is a Book. There are sacraments. There are oil and bread and wine. The minister sits on four thousand years of tradition available for support and encouragement. There is even merit in faithfully going through the motions. Let me repeat: When I am dying, I want a priest who knows what to do. I do not want an amateur psychologist.

The Image of the Disabled

Occasionally we have a service at Grace Cathedral to celebrate the ministries of the disabled. At that service I catch a glimpse of the heart of ministry that I rarely see in any other context. The disabled hold a mirror up to us all. They force us to ask awkward questions about what we truly love. What is the right way to behave toward other human beings? How are persons supposed to be treated? How is power exercised in God's Kingdom?

Think of the insult behind the words *disabled* and *impaired* in our culture. We have already taken a look at the burden of words on the ordained. We ministers carry hopes and aspirations for others. We are called to be more virtuous than others. We are supposed to live by higher standards. We shouldn't complain. It goes with the territory, but knowing it doesn't make it any easier. Where is the true focus of pastoral identity? The mystery of disablement and impairment raises the question of what we are really about, what a human being is for. Disablement is a prism through which we can discern the mystery of the gospel, because we are all disabled, impaired, and broken in some way.

I want to give two examples of impairment and brokenness that might help us understand the ordained ministry better. The first is contemporary, the second is taken from recent history—the treatment of tuberculosis from about 1850 to 1950.

The Revolution of the Deaf

On 9 March 1988 there was a revolution of the deaf. The students at a special college for the deaf were up in arms. The headlines read, "Strike at Gallaudet" and "Students Demand a Deaf President." The seeds of this revolution were sown in 1817 by Laurent Clerc, a French writer and teacher who was born deaf, who founded the American Asylum for the Deaf in Hartford, Connecticut, with Thomas Gallaudet. Clerc was the spiritual leader of the world community of the deaf until he died in 1869. He asked, "Is deafness a disability to be fought tooth and nail, or is it to be graciously accepted?" We might well pose this question with regard to our own limitations and weaknesses. When do we fight? When do we submit?

Laurent Clerc helped resolve the question by widening people's idea of human nature. He refused to be straitjacketed by what was commonly thought of as "normal." He had a deep sense of the generous and wide range of "nature" and of our call to respect this range even when we don't understand it. He wrote, "Every creature, every work of God, is admirably made. What we find faulty in its kind turns to our advantage without our knowing it. . . . We can only thank God for the rich diversity of his creation." He sensed himself and other deaf people "as different but nonetheless complete beings." As Oliver Sacks wrote, Clerc's view of God and his world is "humble, appreciative, and unresentful." In contrast, Sacks cites the example of Alexander Graham Bell, who constantly saw "deafness as a swindle and a privation and a tragedy." He wanted to "normalize" the deaf, "correct" God's blunders, and in general "improve on" nature. "Clerc argues for cultural richness, tolerance, diversity. Bell argues for technology, for genetic engineering, hearing aids, telephones. The two types are wholly opposite but both clearly have their parts to play in the world."[11]

This might explain some of the rage and even resentment found in many a minister, particularly those of a reforming nature. If one tries to minister in the midst of great poverty and injustice, the temptation to "correct God's blunders" is sometimes irresistible. Outrage has a time and place, but it can also occasion shipwreck. Many clergy become inflated with self-righteousness on behalf of the poor and the oppressed. Rage at injustice can so hook into some ministers' lust for power, to count for something, to be noticed, and to be right that it paradoxically ruins them. Yet I often wonder if our sisters and brothers are sometimes ruined on our behalf because we are too afraid to take a stand?

Ministers, because they live from the place of deepest weakness, identify with struggles such as the revolution of the deaf not out of being committed to a political agenda but by reason of knowing that they belong to a common humanity. Such it is to be God's fool.

Blaming the Ill

The second example of impairment and brokenness is the history of the treatment of tuberculosis. It too throws some light on the ordained ministry as the celebration of the solidarity of all human beings. Until the late nineteenth century, tuberculosis was considered morally neutral. It often attacked brilliant, amorous, and doomed poets. But then it began to be considered a disease of dirty and untalented reprobates. "Tubercle attacks failures," wrote an "expert" in 1912, and punitive treatments were developed that reflected the belief that "the beautiful and rich receive it from the unbeautiful poor." The results for society were incalculably destructive. Even after Robert Koch isolated the bacillus in 1882, for two decades most people in Britain refused to accept the simple medical explanation for the disease's infectiousness. "Experts" blamed such things as masturbation, cocktails, and waltzing for causing tuberculosis. Tobacco wasn't condemned because too many doctors smoked.

I can't help seeing a parallel in my own training as a priest. Like physicians and therapists, clergy often work in the dark and mistrust what we don't understand or can't explain away. Repressive mythologies and "New Age" remedies grow up around things we do not understand or do not want to know. Clergy often become peddlars of these mythologies and remedies, as ways of "curing" what is beyond our understanding.

When it came to tuberculosis, doctors were baffled by it and appalled by their ineffectuality. They indulged in the practice of radical but useless surgery. One doctor in the 1860s claimed that boa constrictor excreta gave instantaneous relief. (Such a remedy doesn't sound too remote from California in the 1990s!) As the nineteenth century progressed, some doctors, desperate for an explanation, became convinced that tubercular diseases were caused by a moral weakness in the sufferer—a liking for idle amusements, sexual indulgence, and even "nostalgia." The illness became a disgrace as well as a disease.

The same punitive spirit is alive and well today in the way we judge each other psychologically. We sum each other up knowingly, as if a human being could be reduced to a few symptoms. The incurably ill patients of the past not only felt bad themselves but made those trying to cure them feel bad. They were blamed for being sick. "The casually inflicted unhappiness . . . was the result of human imagination being deliberately stunted, of physicians running away from the painful emotions that surround physical pain, of fears that medical authority would be overwhelmed if it acknowledged the private misery of tuberculosis."[12] It is not difficult to transpose this to the diseases of the soul and to the way priests and ministers in the past have dealt with them. Parodies and caricatures of Catholic or Protestant childhoods abound. The wounding guilt leaves its mark in the large numbers of lapsed Catholics and Protestants brutalized by early indoctrination. Witness the growing movement of Fundamentalists Anonymous. We still foster alienating conditions today. Through the centuries the clergy have always had ways of making people feel inferior or even subhuman in the name of God. It is hardly surprising that so many people have abandoned organized religion and think of priests and ministers as either dangerous or irrelevant.

These two examples of the deaf and of the treatment of tuberculosis raise the question of what it is to be human. This question is at the heart of ministry.

Being Human: The Cycle of Death and Resurrection

What is a person? The Bible shows two contradictory aspects of what it is to be human. We are enslaved and free, broken and healed, fallen and destined for glory. The Fall is the primordial myth of our brokenness. In Saint Paul we hear of the unending glory that is our destiny. Christ is the *Spannungsmensch*, the stretched-out man (to use Rudolf Bultmann's famous expression). We, like Christ, are stretched out between our fallenness and our glory.

In the third chapter of Genesis we read the myth of the Fall. The fall into what? In some interpretations the Fall is the wound of knowledge. It is our "fall" into existence, into being itself. We become subject to time and necessity and realize that we are part of "the cycle of dung and death." We are enslaved to a rhythm of endless and pointless repetition. This is the Fall. We see it in personal relations and in world politics. It is the strange and terrible guilt that some experience in simply being alive.

By itself the Fall is a cruel and debilitating myth. But taken with the story of our glory, it becomes a fruitful myth that helps us understand our pain and find an antidote. God looks for Adam and Eve in the Garden of Eden. Human beings were and are made to be companions of God. "Where are you?" asks God. And until human beings find their identity in God, they live by a pattern of shame and blame.

Many a priest perpetuates the pattern of death. The man blames the woman, and the woman, the serpent. Thus we become dislocated. We are out of place and lost. We find ourselves in the "region of unlikeness," cut off from ourselves, one another, and God. The terrible mystery of sin is that we can be unlike ourselves if we so choose. The Fall involves our being able to harness the energy of death and use it against others.

The primary vocation of ministers with regard to their sense of self is to be earthed, to be as humanly human as they know how. We are called to help people find their way home, and we cannot do this unless we are at home with ourselves.

In 2 Cor. 4:7–14 Saint Paul celebrates our resurrection in the Spirit. Here the resurrection is the reversal of the Fall. There is, thank God, an energy working in us other than that of our fallenness. It is one that is always preparing us for the "weight of glory." This extraordinary phrase aptly describes our pilgrimage.

Yet the myth of the Fall still informs much of our lives. In the Gospel of Mark (3:20–35) Jesus is accused of casting out demons by the power of Beelzebul. The same kind of accusations are thrown around today. Think of our false naming of people and things. We abuse each other when we abuse language. Thank God we live in a world where the deaf have spoken to us, where those ill with the unnameable and unacceptable minister to us. The love we receive is God's folly, and we are God's fools. The wild inclusiveness of the Body of Christ enables us to tell the truth and use language accurately. In the fellowship of all God's people, we are not likely to call terrorists "freedom fighters" or right-wing dictatorships "democracies." We are not likely to mistake "the law of the jungle" for the freedom of the individual.

What kind of God do you serve? What kind of human being would this God create? God and those who minister in his name stand as a contradiction to our cruel Darwinian society, the motto of which is "It's just too bad if you can't make it." Jesus calls us into a wider and more inclusive reality by asking, "Who are my mother and my brothers and sisters?" We are one family, a priestly people. We recognize all people as our mothers and fathers, sisters and brothers.

We say we are the Body of Christ, and that's exactly what we are— together. We are made the Body of Christ by the Body of Christ, by the bread and wine we consecrate and receive in the sacrament of Holy Communion. The healing power of Christ enables us to listen to particular needs of all kinds of people—the physically challenged, the mentally anguished, and the spiritually hungry. Why? Because they are our sisters and brothers. We are all one under the skin.

Saint John of the Cross insisted that "in the end we shall be examined in love." That's it! That's all. To be a minister is to be in the service of that love forever—God's fool.

The priest in Francis MacManus's novel *The Greatest of These* describes the foolishness of ministry very well. "If a man were to deliver all his goods to feed the poor and deliver his body to be burned and have not charity, it profits him nothing. Yes! that's not just catechism stuff. It works in everything. . . . They say, Ned, that faith moves mountains. But you could pull the stars down with love."[13] Pulling down the stars with love! What could be more foolish than that?

CHAPTER FOUR

Nurturing the Broken Minister

In J. F. Powers's novel *Wheat That Springeth Green,* the priest Joe Hackett says, "After years of trying to walk on the water . . . it's good to come ashore and feel the warm sand between my toes."[1] And when theater director Peter Brook writes of "the soul-destroying effect of doing the same job often and too long,"[2] I cannot help but think that the same applies to the ordained as to actors. Many clergy are like actors playing the same old role in the same old play. I realize that I am, like an actor, "merely" symbolic for large numbers of people. I am larger than life. This is dangerous both for me and for those who see me in that way, unless we are grounded in a tradition that sustains us all.

Sometimes I am symbolic of something dull, stupid, and dangerous. I stand as a representative of a deadly and dependably wrong tradition. For others I represent something strong and healing. To their credit, enough people can distinguish between the symbol and the person so that I am not trapped forever in their negative or positive projections.

Everyone wears a mask or a persona (like an actor). This is good. We could not live in the world without them. We all play roles that are necessary for life to go on. But we get into trouble when we are unable to lay the role aside and take off the mask. A minister's inability to set aside his or her persona always leads to absurdity or tragedy. Perhaps that is why so many of us mess up and need looking after. Too much is put on us and we cave in. We take too much on and find ourselves drained and empty. We mistake exposing people inappropriately to our inner psychic drama for true openness and vulnerability. The "people in the pew" are partly responsible. They get the clergy they deserve. They, after all, are ministers too.

Why Clergy Break Down

In my attempt to make sense of my own weakness as an ordained minister and as a human being, I began to recover something of the fire that set me off on the path of ordination in the first place. The problems of the ordained often begin long before ordination, with false expectations and a cruel and demanding idealism. Many of us suffer from a crippling duality of a low self-image coupled with high ideals. We find it difficult to reach out, and clergy are often notorious for their unwillingness or inability to look after one another. More often than not, clergy breakdown is constellated around issues of intimacy (sometimes, but not always, sexual).

I have known clergy (especially the idealistic ones) who feel trapped in their bodies. Those struggling to be celibate and to play a black-suited role in the community often burst headlong out of their prison in the effort to connect with another human being. When I lived in New York, I would hear of ministers who would slip out of their uniforms and into their jeans and go cruising anonymously in Greenwich Village looking for connections. For one brief damaging and inappropriate moment they would imagine themselves held and loved. It would then be time to return to the isolating prisonhouse of the ordained ministry. With help, many clergy have been able to make the journey back into their bodies and find ways to be intimate that are not destructive.

We need help sorting out the difference between our inner selves and our roles. People expect us to be mother, father, husband, wife, and lover. When our unacknowledged need connects with another's projection onto us, both of us pay heavily.

What adds to the burden of ministry in this delicate area of intimacy and sexuality is the cheap psychologizing of clergy, therapists, and other professionals who get sexually involved with their people, patients, or clients. Clergy should certainly be confronted with their behavior and be made accountable. Great damage is done when self-destructive behavior, whether with sex or substance abuse, is swept under the carpet. Too often clergy problems are "solved" by shipping the minister to another community, where the same pattern of behavior is repeated. On the other hand, clergy are sometimes confronted and made accountable in an openly vindictive or subtly diminishing way. Confrontation is always something of a power play, when someone has "got" something on someone else.

Psychology is a valuable tool to help us understand ourselves and each other, but it is often used to reduce people to manageable categories: George *is* an alcoholic; Susan *is* overweight; Eric *is* compulsive in his sexuality. George, Susan, and Eric are much more than their addictions and cannot be reduced to the banalities of pop psychology. That's why the merely psychological approach is often diminishing. Psychology should be a servant to help uncover the spiritual longings of those who suffer in these ways.

The Morale of the Clergy

In 1989 the National Conference of Catholic Bishops in the United States issued a report, "Reflections on the Morale of Priests." A similar report could be written about the Protestant clergy. The report "is a powerful argument against anyone's considering the ordained ministry in the Roman Catholic Church."[3] Some pictures of the priest can be depressing. In a cycle of booze, golf, and television, relieved by saying mass and being caught up with the trivia of parish life, the priest gets on with it the best he can. One is either a priest of the old school, depressed and alcoholic, or of the new—socially "relevant" and bursting with psychobabble.

Twentieth-century novelists have described the modern priest's inner and outer worlds only too well. J. F. Powers, the author of *Wheat That Springeth Green,* has been described unfairly as a kind of literary anthropologist, "giving us an affectionate portrayal of a down-at-the-heels subculture, his seedy priests like once mighty medicine men of a tribe now relegated to the reservation, its rituals mainly of interest as representations of the past."[4] The archbishop in Powers's novel knew how to make "therapeutic" appointments: "A lush in the suburbs who'd lost his driver's license could find himself walking the corridors of a five-hundred-bed hospital in the city as a chaplain under the thumb of nuns; a big spender could find himself operating under the buddy or the commissar system, with an assistant empowered to act for him and the parish in all money matters over two dollars and fifty cents."[5]

The Roman Catholic Bishops' report refers to "the fragile psychological state of a number of candidates to the priesthood in the Western world," and, we might add, of those who are presently priests and ministers. The "modern character," to quote the same document, "is largely distinguished by the rejection of absolute norms and a reference to the past as a source of wisdom; it is marked by an individualism and subjectivism, a reduction of all things to technology and to the principle of efficiency, a pursuit of 'novelty' and secularization in general."[6] If modernity is the state of affairs in which nothing is sacred, then there is no need of clergy. But even "modernity" is out of date. We live in a postmodern age.

The Postmodern World
of Do-It-Yourself Religion

It is not always easy to tell who or what is breaking down. Is it the minister, or is it the society? Being a minister in a world that sees the human condition as something fleeting, human history as merely a jumble of isolated and disconnected events, and human "truths" arbitrary and plural presents challenges and opportunities: challenges because it is hard to hang on to a different viewpoint when the prevailing one seems obvious to the majority; opportunities because postmodernism, in one sense, is an accurate representation of the biblical vision of the fallenness of the human condition and thus opens up the possibility for healing and redemption.

In our society we are encouraged to write our own scripts and make up our own meanings. We have the freedom to choose almost any kind of life we want but are enslaved because we do not have the spiritual maturity or skill to discriminate, to know how to choose one thing over another. Everything goes because nothing really matters. Religion, like everything else, becomes just a matter of taste. Ministers of religion are its purveyors. People are managed by those who claim to know what they really want and are herded together by those who would exploit their inarticulate longings and needs.

We cannot help but understand ourselves (at least in part) in reaction to the postmodernist viewpoint. The way we think of money and how we produce, distribute, and exchange goods and services are intimately related to the way we busily pay attention to constructing ourselves and developing projects for our lives. We used to believe that reality was something tough and solid. Now the assumption is that there are no foundations after all. Our only course is to find accommodation with chronic indeterminacy.[7]

The Lack of Theological Support and the Absence of Prayer

There's an old saying that only two things will save the world: thought and prayer; the trouble is that the people who think don't pray, and those who pray don't think. There are ministers who find themselves on the opposite sides of a great chasm—a chasm of postmodernity. One side clings to a rigid certainty, while the other insists that nothing can be known for certain. Some even go so far as to infer "that meaning is undecidable, indecipherable, and indeterminate; and that ideas of religious revelation are ludicrous. . . . The modern era is undergoing collapse and disintegration; its wounds, mortal; its illness, terminal. These are conditions that give rise to desperate, even dangerous endeavors to preserve and maintain previous stabilities and sensibilities."[8] No wonder some ministers fall apart or retreat into rigid orthodoxies. I am amazed not so much by the fact that so many ministers fall apart as by the fact that so many of them don't. The churches are divided. Some continue to insist that there is an unchanging reality, there are solid foundations, there are fundamental truths. Others seem to have embraced the relativizing attitudes of postmodernism.

A third way, grounded in the mystical tradition of Christianity, acknowledges the temporary nature of all human formulations yet insists that the grace and love of God are foundations that can be trusted. Many priests and pastors are caught between two conflicting worldviews and seem unaware that the path to reconciliation is through the door of spirituality and prayer.

The priest in J. F. Powers's novel "no longer hoped for a break-through, no longer forced himself to meditate, lest God and he both be bored."[9] Meanwhile, what do we do with our pain? Is every life marked by immeasurable and half-concealed suffering? What is it that enables us to feel our pain to the full and so liberate us to live through it gracefully? It is hard for a minister to admit that he or she is spiritually bankrupt. We find it hard voluntarily to take the inner life seriously. It sometimes takes a crisis to bring us to our knees.

The Fear of Experience

Ministers seem to fear experience, ecstasy, what the tradition calls the experiential knowledge of God. Over the years several people have come to me hurt, confused, and outraged because they had had a deep religious experience and had gone to their pastor to talk about it. In every case the pastor referred them to a psychiatrist or therapist. Direct experience is too much for many clergy to handle. It embarrasses them. It makes them feel inadequate. Some of us have an inferiority complex about our relationship with God. Hence a basic conflict may arise at the core of our ministry when we suppress what we should love.

Broken by a False Vision

One of the myths of the modern era is that human beings are rational and act reasonably. We take for granted the idea that human beings are atomic units. Is it any wonder that people latch on to the minister (even the most feebly charismatic) because they experience themselves free but bored? The question is, Do people want to "find themselves" or "lose themselves" in a charismatic personality or community?

Some ministers are taken in and taken up by other people's view of them. They begin to believe that they possess the gifts of the Spirit and can therefore do no wrong. The rules do not apply to them. They become victims of a false transcendence. One thinks of a Jim Jones or a Charles Manson. They believed that their obsessions were divinely inspired. "There is really only One and we are all part of that One" and other such banalities are the stock in trade of ministers enthralled with themselves.

In such cases the breakdown of ministers is sincerely to be preferred to their acting out the obsession in their disciples. Manson and Jones are extreme cases, but ministers easily take too much on to themselves.

More modest breakdowns do, of course, occur—ones that are hardly visible. Some clergy think of themselves as part of a small and select band of the really faithful and prophetic—apostolic snobs. Joe Hackett, J. F. Powers's priest, remonstrates with his new curate: "Pride. You look down your nose at people out here because they aren't poor. They aren't poor enough, good enough, or maybe bad enough, to have you for a priest."[10]

I suppose we're all frightened, and we look for ways to feel safe and superior. I wonder how many of us realize that our anxieties are well founded. It is ludicrous to think that we and we alone are called to take on burdens impossible to bear. I find that my present job as dean of a large cathedral is truly "impossible." My spirituality is shaped by Alcoholics Anonymous in that my impossible situation invites me to "live one day at a time." When I remember to do that, it's very liberating.

Leadership by Means of the Centered, Unafraid Self

The loss of the clergy's status and the change in moral standards have left ministers without a clear model for leadership. As I was growing up, I can remember meeting kindly elderly clergy who seemed to be at a loss. They had been formed as priests in England before the Second World War. When that war was over, they were left high and dry—anachronisms, sometimes saintly and often silly, in a world that had left them behind. They were no longer treated with respect. There was a time in the United States when a priest would be called to the front of the line, excused the fare on the bus, or given a 10 percent discount. It is not that these little perks and signs of recognition were important in themselves; but they did indicate a widespread attitude of respect that contrasts sharply with the public's estimation of the clergy today. The model was different and the culture has changed. One of J. F. Powers's priests thinks about what it used to be like to be ordained. "We used to stand out in the crowd. We had quality control. We were the higher-priced spread. No more."[11]

People do need leaders, however. Such a need isn't infantile; it's normal. Leadership in the Church is not so much a matter of acquiring skills as developing a centered spirituality of presence. Ministers need to be so committed to their own spiritual journeys, and the truth telling it involves, that they can learn to be centered and still in the middle of raging storms.

Help Is Never Far Away, But Who Will Seek It?

Part of me wants to say that it doesn't matter much what ministers do to get help as long as they do something! The body, mind, and spirit all need attention. How many clergy look after their bodies? Exercise? Massage? How many grasp the many opportunities to read and to think, to take continuing education courses? How many are engaged in a serious program of spiritual growth? I have been led unwillingly into looking after myself by the threat of one disaster or another. It often takes a crisis to bring our attention to areas of gross physical, mental, and spiritual neglect. Many churches need to recover the ministry of healing, starting with the minister.

Everyone, especially the ordained, needs a friend of the soul against whom he or she can test for reality. Over the years I have had various forms of therapy; I also have an ongoing relationship with a spiritual director. I make my confession regularly. I am open to offerings of continuing education. I have been led kicking and screaming into seminars on such things as conflict management and family systems. There is plenty of help available for the minister, not least from such excellent organizations as the Alban Institute in Washington, D.C.[12]

Sometimes it's hard to persuade ministers to slow down and take time out for refreshment and healing. A good friend of mine contributed to my sanity recently by making a simple suggestion. "Go through your calendar and every week strike out a day with a pencil—a day other than your day off. You need some free, unstructured time in your life. You'll still do some work on those days, but they won't get filled up unless you choose to fill them." I know advice is cheap. In this case it worked because my friend's timing was perfect. But many clergy don't know how to look for help and resent it when it is offered.

Another form of resistance is a closed mind and a fearful heart with regard to new ideas and techniques. Some condemn everything that can be labeled New Age, in much the same way that I was told by a frightened nun, years ago, that yoga was of the devil. The intellectual among us make fun of the self-help industries and thus avoid what they have to teach.

I'm not asking that we become uncritical but that we be open to what other traditions (particularly healing ones) are trying to tell us. When I can afford it, I have a massage. I find that it has a good effect not only on my body but also on my mind and heart. The massage therapists often talk what sounds to me like metaphysical gobbledygook. That doesn't matter, because the result is clearly sane and good.

A fundamental and traditional principle is at work here. Much of popular Christianity is "unnatural"—it doesn't build on nature. It by-passes nature by insisting on a very narrowly understood conversion experience. Nature, politics, the mysteries of the body, mind, and spirit are left outside. This is why there is often something unreal and ungrounded about people's religion. It doesn't touch their day-to-day lives. The old principle is "Grace does not destroy nature but perfects it." Christianity builds on what God has already given us. We lose a great deal when we refuse to look (albeit with a critical eye) at the healing possibilities open to us.

The Clergy's Fear of Intimacy

Many clergy find it difficult to trust the laity. J. F. Powers's priest thought to himself, "But then, running a parish, any parish, was like riding in a cattle car at winter time—you could appreciate the warmth of your dear, dumb friends, but you never knew when you'd be stepped on, or worse."[13] The maturity of a congregation is tested when its minister falls apart. Some congregations have a reputation for chewing up their pastors and then spitting them out. Others seem able to cope with ministerial failure with humanity and grace. Too few congregations know *how* to help their ministers even when they know that their ministers need nurturing.

How much harder it is when clergy are closed off from others. Our capacity for mutual self-deception seems to know no bounds. Are we drawn to become ministers (counselors) precisely at the point when chaos threatens? Doesn't my being ordained help to make me unreachable by distancing me from my own internal struggles? I am often further distanced by being placed in unequal relationships, in which I have access to other people's frailties without having to disclose my own.[14]

You see the danger the minister is in. We are led away from the promise and possibility of intimacy and are often seduced by "promiscuous access to other people's inadequacy and suffering."[15] The appetite for personal influence can be all-consuming, especially when we tell ourselves that it is to help others. With the best of intentions, ministers enlarge themselves and feel superior by helping others.[16] It is sobering to reflect that the word *therapist* also can be written as *the rapist*.

I was often tormented by the thought that as a priest I was really up to no good. The voice inside me, judging me, was very harsh on this point, and there was sufficient external evidence to make me believe it for a while. After all, I wasn't perfect, and there were witnesses! The clergy often harbor a secret fear and contempt of their congregations. The congregation is the enemy, the mob that always asks for a golden calf to worship. No wonder the minister often collapses out of "compassion fatigue."

Clergy:
Neurotics and Psychopaths?

One reason for the conflict not only in a minister's personal life but also between clergy and congregations is the tension between who the ministers are in themselves and who they are called to be on behalf of others. In the wake of the apparent triumph of Freud and the psychoanalysts who followed him, many ministers have swallowed the view that religious experiences are merely expressions of defense mechanisms at best or severe psychopathology at worst. Clergy undermine their own calling by doubting its very validity. Clergy are revealed to be human after all. But this often implies that being human is a terrible weakness that drains ministers of any power or authority. Ministers and priests, along with "yogis, saints, shamans, and sages have all been chopped down to neurotic size."[17] There is no room for grace. All we are left with is human frailty and pathetic psychological weakness. Thank God we are gradually moving away from this psychological reductionism, but the tendency over the years to denigrate and pathologize religious experiences and practices has hurt many of the clergy.

What Roger Walsh writes about the way shamans have been understood in history in *The Spirit of Shamanism* can also be applied to clergy. We are either frauds or sinless beings. Shamans were diagnosed and dismissed "as merely neurotic or psychotic, charlatans or con men. On the other hand, popular writers often portray them as superhuman saints or sages."[18] Great and unreasonable expectations are put on public figures and celebrities. Whoopi Goldberg, a talented actress and comedienne of whom much is expected, tried to reclaim her ordinariness recently by pointing out that she wasn't a cure for cancer.

Clergy aren't cures for anything either. They are the willing and unwilling carriers of a deep need in human beings, the need for "the madness of God"—ecstasy. They are those chosen to affirm that humanity is related to the infinite. They are supposed to know the famous maxim "Man without God is no longer man": "Humanity without God is no longer human." Many are crushed by the burden of being disconnected from God and from each other. Who would dare to claim to be someone set apart to serve, heal, and enlighten? Who would dare to claim to be a sign of the untapped power of God in everyone?

Yet the expectation that clergy be in touch with a deeper reality is not entirely unreasonable. This is part of the job description, and we shouldn't whine about it. It is hard, however, to be called to point to another dimension of reality in a society that on the whole denies its existence. This is but another instance of the cycle of sacrifice and delight. It can be seen in the "burden of ministry" in the service of the One whose yoke is easy and whose burden is light. It can be discerned in the pain and promise in the expectations of others who long to be connected with God and with each other. Sacrifice and delight are found in what I can only call the painful and joyful "humiliation of grace." Grace humbles the self-sufficient empty self in us and gives radiance to the self who knows its need of God.

When the Minister Sins

The Church is notoriously bad about handling the weaknesses and sins of its ordained ministers. One hears of congregations missing opportunities to confront, forgive, and restore many a pastor. No one is to blame for this failure to heal and to reconcile. We are all at fault. We all resist the promise of the gospel. We are deaf to the Word. We also do not know how to look after ourselves and to minister to one another.

We are captive to and victims of the prevailing therapeutic metaphors of the age. We easily get labeled. The labels give brief comfort, and we quickly look around for explanations of our pain. Certainly pathologies are fashionable (this is not to deny their validity)—I must be the way I am because I am the adult child of an alcoholic, or because I was sexually abused as a child. These sad and crippling truths do not exhaust who I am. I am also God's delight, and concentrating on "explanations" of our pain blinds us to the deeper truth about ourselves.

I think of the pastor who waited thirty-two years to unburden himself of his guilt over kissing a neighbor's wife. Another minister, recently widowed, was overcome by confusion and guilt because he experienced an erection while he was stroking his dog. One priest found himself smelling excrement on the altar when he celebrated the eucharist. A fiercely conservative minister, living in the suburbs, every six weeks or so would slip into the city for a one-night stand. I think of the sexually attractive woman who dresses well and is obviously happy with her body, whose very attractiveness is used as a weapon against her by her fellow ministers, both male and female (the men nervous or sexist, the women envious or hostile). Another woman denies her femininity in the name of a feminism that is both joyless and humorless. There are many ways delight is suppressed and denied.

Many of us have neither the inner resources nor the means of asking for help with regard to our passions and longings. If we feel untouched by any of these problems, we might ask ourselves how much wildness and passion there is in us? Have we lost our capacity for delight? How far have we fallen away from our first love?

The Healing Game of Being Awake

One of the best ways to understand the spiritual life is to think of it as a game. The word *game* may come as a bit of a surprise, but the clergy are part of a tradition of "tricksters" who have, with varying success, been called to wake people up to a different view of the world. The word *game* doesn't imply anything trivial or frivolous. Here it means something deeply significant, "namely the choice to confront meaningful challenges that test and hone our abilities as we strive for cherished goals. . . . Without meaningful games we languish in boredom and meaninglessness."[19] The question is, What kind of game is worth playing? The answer is, The game of being awake, the game of sacrifice and delight. There is nothing more important than this game. The other four games we play—money, power, sex, and status—are trivial and insignificant compared with this one. Clergy get as caught up in these trivial games as anyone. When we get drawn into all four games, we may experience moral and even physical breakdown.

The following conversation might well be instructive to clergy when they worry about what they are, what they are for, what game they are called to play.

> "Are you a God?" they asked the Buddha. "No," he replied.
> "Are you an angel, then?" "No."
> "A saint?" "No."
> "Then what are you?"
> Replied the Buddha, "I am awake."

Some have called this game of wakefulness the Master Game. "It still remains the most demanding and difficult of games, and in our society, there are few who play."[20]

Learning to Be in Two Places at Once

One of the problems with the clergy is that many think they have been ordained to preach and to deal with the known rather than having been commissioned to explore the unknown. Priests and ministers have to learn to be in two places at once, spiritually speaking. They have to be grounded in the tradition of which they are the representatives. At the same time they have to be pioneers of the uncharted and unknown. They have to represent their tradition and transcend it simultaneously. Their training should be a process of detribalization, of a maturing and ever more inclusive vision—a worldview that loves and reveres all creatures as part of one great web of life. In this context, doubt is as much a part of the minister's armory as faith.

The crisis of vocation is surely a crisis of faith. Should I answer the call to journey, like Abraham and Sarah, into the untried and unknown, or should I stay where I am, with the known and the familiar? Abraham Maslow puts it well. "If you deliberately plan to be less than you are capable of being, then I warn you that you will be deeply unhappy for the rest of your life."[21] Albert Camus wrote, "When a man has learned—and not on paper—how to remain alone with his suffering, how to over-come his longing to flee, then he has little left to learn."[22] How many of us of the clergy have been helped to learn such things? How many of us see our vocation in these terms? If we did, we would experience deeper sacrifice. If we did, we would enjoy a greater delight.

Liberated for Community and Communion

There is a simple spiritual truth: When we know how to be alone with our suffering, when we are given the grace not to run away, we are then liberated for community and communion. We begin to love our neighbors as ourselves. We see every living thing in this neighborly way. But this is no longer a nice spiritual maxim. It is a vital necessity, because the planet is in crisis. Roger Walsh writes that "we are engaged in a race between consciousness and catastrophe." He goes on, "Each person we meet, every situation, every interaction, presents us with a choice. We choose whether to see ourselves apart from others or whether to look past the otherness to the self we share. . . . It is not a minor choice. The way we choose to see ourselves and our relationship to the world may decide its fate and ours."[23]

What a wonderful enterprise with which to be identified as minis-ters of good news. In the struggle to choose and to choose life—to choose to be awake—we find ourselves in the gracious cycle of sacrifice and delight.

A friend writes that the minister is "a representative of a spiritual community, a person who symbolically and functionally represents a spiritual presence/opportunity. . . . I'm impressed with the harsh real-ity that my profession is filled with hurting Pastor/parish relation-ships. . . . We are in danger of losing our sense of calling because we are so overwhelmed and undercared for in the midst of this human suffering and need."[24]

Ordinary Remedies: Friendship and Love

Our ordinary needs are met in ordinary ways, but we have to *ask*. Our ministry is made of earthy material. We start with a common humanity, with common longings and common wounds. Being a minister requires the ordinary stuff of friendship and love. Ned Langton, the bishop in Francis MacManus's *Greatest of These,* thought of his ruined and lonely priest, half-mad with longing. A man needed the "warm virtues like friendship and kindness, for his own sake even more than for the sake of others, because if he wasn't warmed by them . . . he needed the furnace that the mystics knew, the gift of vision face-to-face that was transcendent super-human life, or else he became a naked animal raging with the cold and with his own released wildness."[25]

We must find ways of letting the blood flow through our veins. All of us have our peculiarities and particularities, our vulnerabilities, impairments, and disabilities. We all live with issues around which pride and fear are constellated. Friendship, spiritual direction, prayer, relaxation, the ability to have fun and to give ourselves to others save us from being suffocated and overcome by a sense of failure, seduced by the voice inside us that tells us we are no good. Like everyone else, ministers exhibit both the self-pity of the afflicted and the indifference of the privileged.

A psychiatrist friend once told me of a woman suffering from anorexia nervosa. She would bring to every session a bag of doughnuts and beg him to eat them. Starving herself, she was obsessed with food. I think of many a priest and pastor as suffering from a kind of spiritual anorexia. Starved spiritually, we seek to force-feed others. We need to be fed ourselves before we can feed others.

Yet this is not strictly true. There is "the miracle of the empty hands" in Georges Bernanos's *Diary of a Country Priest.* Having ministered in a perfunctory way to a dying and difficult parishioner, the priest sees that she died in peace. He looks at his empty hands and marvels that he is able to give to others what he himself does not possess. "'Be at peace,' I told her. And she had knelt to receive this peace. May she keep it forever. It will be I that gave it her. Oh, miracle—thus to be able to give what we ourselves do not possess, sweet miracle of our empty hands."[26]

CHAPTER FIVE

The Context of Ministry:
Religion in the
Twenty-first Century

T he religious scene in the United States has long been a source of wonderment and amusement. We are a sectarian and individualistic lot. Our religion looks vulgar, simplistic, and given to extremes. We face enormous social problems: the decay of our cities, the loss of a sense of family and of community, and the expectation that religious groups will continue to provide basic social services in an age of diminishing government programs. We tend to espouse an irresponsible pluralism and adopt a policy of noninterference. Pluralism has come to mean separatism and tribalism.

Two major social trends pose a challenge now and will continue to do so in our religious future: the first, according to Robert Bellah, is an individualism that has grown cancerous; the second is a pluralism, which we value so highly, that is turning sour.[1] Both individualism and pluralism dress up in the plumage of freedom, but in actual fact they often cover up mass indifference and collective irresponsibility. Both are inimical to the idea of human solidarity, of community.

To complicate matters, in spite of the heroic and sometimes paranoid attempts to separate Church and State, religion and politics are inextricably bound up with each other. As we approach the end of the millennium, we can expect the confusion to intensify.

Living in a Deprived Culture

Human beings can't help being products of their culture, and from a spiritual point of view, we live in a deprived one. Jean Sulivan, a French priest and novelist, wrote, "The West is the third world of the spirit. Its sadness can't be fathomed; it's the sadness of those who are separated from themselves, insatiable. The poverty and destitution of the third world still leaves room for fraternity in collective agony. In the West agony is individual. Old and young, sick and handicapped—all are placed in the charge of specialists but are irredeemably alone."[2] We might wonder what the religious future will look like if, indeed, "the West is the third world of the spirit." What is it like for the professionals, the ordained, to live and work in such spiritually deprived circumstances?

We already live in a sort of shopping mall of the spirit. We go shopping for religion in much the same way that we go shopping for anything. Spiritual "goods" are on display in the various churches, temples, and synagogues. We are free to browse along the aisles of the therapeutic and religious supermarket and buy whatever strikes our fancy. Most of us are unaware of the historical and social realities that have determined the way we look at the world; we are under the illusion that we choose our religious beliefs without reference to tradition and history.

It is unlikely that our attitude toward religion will change drastically. In fact there are clear indications that our supermarket/shopping-mall religion will continue to flourish and that the designated "god" persons (ministers) of our fast-food culture will still have their place in this, "the third world of the spirit."

The diseases of the culture are sure to affect the ordained. Church leaders are icons and instances of the diseases of a particular society, and ours is an addictive and acquisitive one. We tend to get the spiritual leaders we deserve. They are often as spiritually impoverished as we are. They are us.

The Absence of a Sense of History

One of the reasons we face daunting psychological and social problems is that people have little or no sense of history—of their own personal history as well as of a historical perspective stretching over hundreds of years. People are free, free of history and therefore free to be alone, cut off, free to drift. And therefore not really free at all.

The clergy reflect the culture. We breathe the same air (psychological as well as physical) as everyone else. We see the same movies and read the same newspapers and magazines as everyone else. Our lives are not hermetically sealed and protected from "the world."

In an essay "The True Builders of Cities," Mark Helprin writes, "One of the reasons Rome fell was the opposite of why the Church and Islam later were to rise: it was innocent of compelling beliefs."[3] We are now living in a period of history when once again a central conception to hold us all together is lacking. We are struggling to find a common language. We lack the imagination to resonate with associations and meanings when we see, for example, a work of art. We have lost an eye for continuity. According to Mark Helprin, "In medieval times when someone walked into a cathedral or spied the towers of a city, a deep spectrum of emotions, fears, and hopes was triggered in him, and enriched immeasurably what he saw. When these people saw the lights of stained glass, they felt the presence of God. The aesthetics of the structure and everything within were a road to that, not, as they are now, an end in themselves."[4]

It is hard to find common symbols to bring us together. One reason is the poverty of our collective imagination. The symbols we *do* have are apprehended in a shallow and fleeting way—the flag, the ballot-box, and the presidency. The political process is brash, vulgar, and sometimes corrupt. The supermarket approach to religion reveals a lowest-common-denominator consumer spirituality. It's hard to go against the grain and be a minister of the gospel when the culture wants one to be a pedlar of religion suitable for public consumption. In one community in Illinois recently, for example, the only symbol for public display during the Christmas season that the citizens could agree on was Frosty the Snowman.

People Don't Know the Story Anymore

Being an English-American (in contrast to an American Anglophile) means I have been formed by two different cultures "divided by a common language." I find that I am always being pushed into embracing wider allegiances. My faith is continually being stretched.

I live in a particular place (San Francisco) where heroic secularism and individualism, the New Age religions, and the great religious traditions other than Christianity all flourish. Christians don't have a corner on the religious market. In the community where I work, the ecumenical spirit is weak, partly because we are all struggling so hard for money to keep our own particular shop open that we have very little time for each other. Another reason is that the various councils of churches are finding that simply banding together to do "good works" isn't enough anymore to bind people together.

People drift into Grace Cathedral who haven't lapsed from any spiritual tradition. They do not reject Christianity. They do not know enough to reject it. They do not know even the outline of the story. One visitor asked me recently, "Tell me, what exactly did happen on Good Friday?" This ignorance of the story, I understand, is becoming common in Britain too. In David Hare's play *Racing Demon,* one character recalls his first visit to London. He was lonely and afraid and wanted to buy a crucifix. He went into a shop and the girl behind the counter looked puzzled and then produced two crosses and said, "You won't want this one. It's got a little man on it." More and more people have never heard of "the little man" on the cross. This is the world I live in; perhaps it's the world we shall all soon live in. It's not a bad world in which to find oneself an ordained minister, but it's very different from the world in which I grew up.

I don't know what England is like now. If Jack Lively's description of English society is anything to go by, it's not very different from America. "British society is characterized . . . not by undue reverence for the social order but by the absence of any sense of social coherence or mutual obligation, not by over-concern with continuity and stability but by contempt for the past and indifference to any future but the immediate."[5] England (and by extension Europe—in fact, all that we call the West) and America are parts of one culture, increasingly indifferent to or ignorant of Christianity. The times in which we live are full of opportunity as well as stress for the ordained ministry.

What are people like nowadays? What do they feel and think? What can ministers do to serve them? Over the past century there has grown up in the West, and especially in the United States, a vision of the human person (the self) that is almost devoid of historical perspective. The self has a short memory. It has become a cliché to refer to our chronic self-contained individualism. We hesitate to accept that there is no abiding universal "self" but only selves formed by particular times and places. In this context, no basic, fundamental, pure human nature exists outside history and culture.

Every human being is the product of a particular cultural and historical context. England made me—a particular England, the England of 1940 to 1960. It has left its indelible mark. Think of Aeschylus, Saint Augustine, Muhammad, Zelda Fitzgerald, and Jim Jones all having a conversation about what it means to be human.[6] Further, imagine them discussing a key text from the New Testament, say John 3:16, "God so loved the world . . . " What would they make of it?

How to Fill the Empty Self

One way to understand a modern view of the soul is to talk about "the empty self," about a self that is aching to be filled. This is a parody of the ancient idea that from a spiritual point of view, the soul is a vast emptiness that only God can fill in a cycle of sacrifice and delight. For the modern soul, emptiness means absence, absence of community, of tradition, and of shared meanings. Psychologist Philip Cushman suggests that this sense of emptiness manifests itself in "a lack of personal conviction and worth, and it embodies the absences as chronic undifferentiated emotional hunger."[7] The cultural triple cure? Advertising, psychotherapy, and religion. The result? We are controlled by those forces that create and manipulate our wish "to be soothed, organized, and made cohesive" by momentarily filling us up. Ministers of religion can easily be caricatured as members of the manipulating elite.

We often experience advertising as a kind of assault. We are attacked for not being like the robust, attractive, and erotically charged people portrayed in the ads. Ads create a problem for us by criticizing who we are at the moment—too fat, too poor, too unglamorous. They go on to offer a product that promises a comprehensive solution. "Buy this, and be rewarded by a new life-style just like that of the model in the ad." If we drink the right brand and wear the right clothes, we will experience a magical transformation into the life-style of which these products are a sign. The pre-Reformation doctrine of transubstantiation looks tame next to the modern magic of advertising. We buy life-style in a vain attempt to effect the miracle of transubstantiation on ourselves. Our lives remain for the most part unsatisfying and unfixable. Religion tends to advertise itself as a "product" that promises specific results, and the ordained are its traveling salespersons.

The advertising industry exists and flourishes because it convinces the public of the transforming power of products. Ads tend to pass on to us not so much information as a feeling, cleverly evoked to suggest that the product somehow actually conjures up happy, healthy, bronzed models. We used to be concerned about building religious "character," with a working and active conscience. The emphasis now is on developing a pleasing personality that knows how to gain approval. We tend to be low on substance and high on appearance. We take short-term opportunistic views to make money. We lose a sense of loyalty and integrity. Religion is co-opted as an adjunct to the self-improvement industry.

Because the empty self is always in need, the "goods" designed to fill it up are never enough. Philip Cushman points to our low self-esteem, our confusion over values, our eating disorders, drug abuse, and chronic consumerism as indicators of the empty self. Religion claims to speak to the inner suffering caused by the absence of a sense of personal worth and by the lack of personal convictions. It knows that neither food nor drugs will fill the emptiness inside us. But religion can become dangerous and manipulative when people turn to it as a sort of final solution, the ultimate consumer trip. They want to consume "God" or the "Truth" as if they were candy bars.

The Web of Meaning

The cure for emptiness offered by advertising is, of course, illusory. Traditional cultures use different tools to provide a web of meaning for the soul in community: "stories, songs, rituals, ceremonial objects, costumes and potions that heal by teaching and readjusting the society's cultural frame of reference."[8] Ads cannot provide a web of meaning, but they can and do offer life-style as a solution. Fantasies can be bought. Many clergy are out of touch with or even unaware of the traditional tools available to them for shifting society's frame of reference in a more healing and communal direction. Many ministers, like many psychotherapists, have swallowed the myth of the empty and insatiable self and try to minister to it. In many ways this is laudable; but it is futile if the context, the frame of reference, isn't addressed as well. It is futile because the consumed and consuming self is never at rest or at home with itself. People in the helping professions are in a bind because we are products (like everyone else) of the conditions that constructed the empty self in the first place.

Clergy, of all people, should know about community and tradition as necessary for locating and grounding the self. To do this we have to be prepared to swim against the tide of the culture and to be signs of contradiction. Isolated, self-contained individuals with no historical sensibility are hardly human. They are already draining away, already driving on empty. They are ripe for exploitation by those in the spiritual transformation industries. My need to be loved, guided, and looked after pushes me into wanting the Church (the minister, the therapist) to be my mother, my father, my lover, mentor, and provider. I set myself up for exploitation or disappointment.

The scarcely human self (according to this model) is always looking for ways to be filled up, whether by food, things, or experiences. One problem, of course, is that the selves we have become require both an uninterrupted flow of money and the continual stimulation to spend it. Psychotherapy wants to help and to heal but is often an agent of perpetuating the very situation it seeks to alleviate.

Our task is to *relocate* the self, with all the particularities of time and place, as a child of God. The preacher and teacher are called to create a context for our transformation that is communal and historical (we tell stories to locate ourselves in time and space). Think of our children and their nurture. Cushman suggests that "perhaps significantly more empathy and accurate reflecting is needed from parents because more traditional sources of guidance have been lost."[9] Who is going to provide an environment that understands empathy, attention, and mirroring? "If adults are self-serving, highly ambitious, heavily bounded individuals, why would they choose to undergo the self-sacrifice and suffering necessary to be nurturing parents?" Why would anyone seek ordination?

The Breakup of the World
We Thought We Knew

Advertising affects our self-understanding by manufacturing imaginary needs and by offering a life-style solution. External upheavals in the world can, however, drastically upset these life-style solutions. The crumbling of a political system in Eastern Europe and in the Soviet Union is a prism through which to look at our own. A theme in the writings of Václav Havel, the president of Czechoslovakia, is the hitherto double life of Eastern Europeans. The totalitarian state demanded signs of outward conformity. All you had to do was keep quiet or, when forced to speak, to use the right words. Hence the double life: systematically saying one thing in public and another in private. Havel saw himself living in a "contaminated moral environment." In his New Year's Day address, he said, "All of us have become accustomed to the totalitarian system, accepted it as an unalterable fact and, therefore, kept it running. . . . None of us is merely a victim of it, because all of us helped to create it together." The crucial "line of conflict," he wrote earlier, did not run between the people and the State but rather through the middle of each person, "for everyone in his or her own way is both a victim and supporter of the system." When I read that sentence, I cannot help but think of many clergy I know. Something has broken inside them, and they have lost the ability and the will to be truthful, even to themselves.

A banner hung above the altar of a church in East Berlin, just after the Berlin Wall came down, read: "I am Cain *and* Abel!" It is hard to imagine many of us coming to a place of such intellectual and spiritual honesty. If only the United States could give up its naive claim to purity and innocence. If only the clergy could come home to themselves and face what's there.

The Crisis of Authority

A few days after the 1989 earthquake in San Francisco there appeared on the streets not only the sellers of T-shirts but the purveyors of religious "explanations." Copies of a pulp paperback were given away on street corners by well-heeled executives. The book laid out God's plan for human history with great authority. The clarity the book offered was very attractive, even if it was phony.

We Americans like authoritative statements, especially if they sound scientific and are uttered by experts. What are the characteristic features of contemporary American culture? We like what "works" in the short term. We like religion to be there but on the sidelines and, in day-to-day terms, irrelevant. Ironically what guides and comforts the popular mind (positivism and the hard "facts" of science) is no longer intellectually defensible. We still like to invoke the authority of "common sense." We also think that straightforward common sense and "hard science" can nail down the truth—what we call the facts. "This doesn't mean we may not have presidents who consult astrologers."

Father Robert Egan points out, "living in a secular culture has its drawbacks. Where nothing is sacred, nothing is holy, nothing is taboo, there is a pervasive flatness of experience, a tendency to get lost in the profane, where nothing is any longer felt to be deeply important, deeply urgent, deeply beautiful, or deeply sad."[10] This flat world seems for many the most real kind of reality. Pastors have to minister to people with flattened and empty souls.

This flatness of soul (what psychologist James Hillman calls our "undernourished, deprived, mute, abused, and violent childishness") began some time ago with our neglect of the city—the *polis*—the commonwealth. We were so caught up in our individualism that we didn't realize that the withering of our institutions meant the diminishment of our souls. We need social institutions to bind us together as a people. We are now apparently unwilling and unable to support them.

On 3 January 1889 philosopher Friedrich Nietzsche collapsed, insane, in the Piazza San Carlo in Turin. He started sending telegrams to his friends, signed either "The Crucified" or "Dionysios." The reasons for his "madness" were physiological, but his craziness is nevertheless powerfully symbolic. Michael Tanner comments, "Nietzsche strikes one as finally blinded by the horrifying clarity of his perceptions of the state we have reached, in which spiritual lethargy and the sense of endless scientific-technological progress combine to provide us with limitless possibilities, and *no* guidelines for preferring some to others."[11]

Much of our nation's intellectual life is pathetically thin. We exchange slogans rather than ideas. We avoid civil discourse and confrontation about the things that matter: sexuality, abortion, the death penalty, defense, foreign policy, the environment, drugs, the poor, the homeless. We do not have a common language, and religion has been reduced to the hobby status of "personal preference." We are not willing to pay the price for our principles. We want values with no personal cost.

Issue-driven by Pressure Groups

We are also a litigious people, often mean and contentious. Issue-ridden pressure groups traumatize the political process and add to our sense of instability. Special-interest groups ignore the maxim "Larger truths include; smaller truths exclude." We go for the smaller truths. This is as true for the life of the churches as it is for society as a whole. As a minister, I am always being pressured to take on the agenda of a particular group. The pressure-group politics of the age (in the Church too) promotes conflict rather than compromise.

We are good at willing the ends but not the means. In opinion polls the large majority of us wants lower taxes: yet in the same polls we approve of spending levels that can be met only by higher taxation. We want lower taxes but not fewer services from the government.

There is an ambivalent attitude in the Constitution of the United States toward religion. It prohibits both the establishment of religion and impediments to its free exercise.[12] It was not the intention of the Constitution to banish religion from the public sphere, yet that is what has happened. As a minister, I often feel stuck with a "religious" label, as defined by the secular culture. The result is that I sometimes feel marginalized and impotent.

What Might the American Religious Future Look Like?

We have seen a dramatic decline of certain denominations associated politically and sociologically with "liberalism," a general withering of the mainline churches, and the sturdy growth of conservative ones. We also live in a time of exceptional religious vigor and are still a very "religious" people. Nevertheless, religious beliefs appear peripheral and private rather than central and integrative. The "private sphere acts as a harmless play area for faith as a leisure-time pursuit."[13]

FOUR POSSIBLE SCENARIOS FOR OUR RELIGIOUS FUTURE[14]

1. *A liberal secular tomorrow* is unlikely. This would assume continuing economic prosperity and the ability of secularism to provide the

ground for national and social values. There is no indication (rather the reverse) that secularism can provide the necessary vitality. The myth that secularization is inevitable runs something like this: Religion is a matter of status anxiety or maladjustment to modernity. The sooner we get over "religion" the better. This myth about the triumph of secularism is now in crisis. Politicians (some sincerely and some opportunistically) are turning to religion in the hope that it will put some spiritual energy into citizens who seem listless and indifferent.

In a society like ours, the State relies on religion for much of its energy and liveliness. People need something to live for. Religion, therefore, isn't likely to die out. What is in question is its *quality* and the quality of its ministers.

2. *Crisis and decline* is a remote possibility. According to this view, religion will become more and more publicly irrelevant, and with negative consequences. There will be a decline of vitality and an ever-weakening leadership. The result? The erosion of the religious and moral underpinnings of the social order and "the slow-motion barbarization of the republic from within."

3. *Apple-pie authoritarianism* is a real possibility. Some would say it is already a reality. It assumes the public relevance of religion but in a negative and repressive manner. Traditional values are invoked to bolster the social order, not because they are true or right but because they are useful. The argument runs something like this: We need a glue to bind society together and the best glue we have is fundamentalist, evangelical Protestantism. It's time more people got on board and made America great again.

4. *Revitalization and renewal* is not impossible. In this scenario the public relevance of religion is affirmed in a positive manner. Religion is not only a narrowly "religious" matter, it is an economic, social, and political one as well. The content of religion is important. If such and such is true (for example, that human beings are made in the image of God), how then should we live? What should our social and political arrangements look like?

What Then Do We Need?

The signs are that power in our society will be very diffuse as the electorate becomes more and more fragmented by one-issue orthodoxies.

Conservatism (of various kinds and not always in harmony with one another) will continue to grow as a political force. What looks like conservatism may be frustration, cynicism, and anger—anger at the excesses of the counterculture. We should also note the division between "moral" and "economic" conservative. The "moral majority" is in conflict with the "me" generation. We shall see confrontation rather than compromise in human relations as this diffused power is exercised. Finally, apathy among voters will be an abiding problem.

What then do we need? Two things. The first is in the realm of ideas. The second has to do with how we construct society.

First, we need to recognize the distinctive relationship of faith and freedom in American history and society. We would then create the conditions for serious and committed public debate. Compelling beliefs are not necessarily the enemy of freedom. It depends on what the beliefs are. Certain compelling beliefs are the condition of freedom.

Second, we need to rejuvenate the so-called mediating structures, those middle-level communities (families, neighborhoods, associations, and so on) that have been vital to American democracy and vitally aided by American religion.[15]

In short, society needs, among other things, a revitalized Church and a renewed ministry. The Church needs to recover both its intellectual and social nerve. The fragmentation in society might not be all bad. It could mean new vitality and new political realignment. On a personal level, however, it can mean confusion and alienation, loss of purpose, fragmented social vision, and the weakening of unifying institutions.

Moving from Compromise to Conviction

We will be an even more high-risk and high-stress society, relieved by leisure and religion. There will be more widespread downward mobility, and the broad middle ground will get narrower as competition increases. Gloomy? Not entirely. The life of faith thrives in times of "the barbarization of culture, vulgarization of politics, trivialization of morals, banalization of art."[16]

One good thing about being a minister who has studied history is that the predictions of our future sound very familiar. We might take note of the following description of Italy at the end of the last century:

"the high hopes of unification degenerated into sordid factionalism, squalid politics, widespread disillusion. An uneasy State faced stubborn provincialism, riotous primitivism and upper-class corruption." Nevertheless, there is a battle of competing values at the heart of our culture. "The *dominant vision* of the next decade will most likely be one of strident individualism lacking the idealism or moral conviction necessary to do more than muddle through."[17]

Can we move from being a culture of compromise to one of conviction? Will the clergy (at least some of them) be the visionaries? The Church and her ministers are the guardians of a vision of human beings who find their identity in their relationship and orientation to boundless mystery, a limitless horizon we call God, and this vision has a transforming impact on our social and political arrangements.

We Need God and We Need Each Other

We are marked by a longing to go beyond ourselves (transcendence) as well as to be truly ourselves (identity). We know that meaningful human life cannot exist apart from relatively stable structures of shared meanings, which nurture community and communion.

Ministers of the liberal churches are often tongue-tied in the presence of their conservative brothers and sisters. We are still too nervous about "absolutes" when it comes to matters of human behavior. G. K. Chesterton asks, "Suppose I say to an employer who exploits workers, 'Slavery suited one stage of evolution.' Suppose he answers, 'And exploitation suits this *stage* in evolution.' There is no response unless there is an absolute test." There is one absolute—the mystery of God, toward whom every human being is oriented. To be human is to be caught up in this mystery in a cycle of sacrifice and delight. To be human is to know that we are blessed and can bless in return.

The secret is *worship*. If we don't find a worthy object, we lapse into idolatry and superstition. Ours is not a time for justifying life-styles but of preaching the conversion of all life-styles in the power of the resurrection. Seen in this light, Christian orthodoxy becomes a romantic adventure.

In short, if there is to be much of a future, we need to be open to conversion, which means a willingness to retrieve the vision of one's own

71

responsibility—a conversion of intellect and will, of mind and heart. The gospel is the good news of God's free gift to us. We respond by becoming responsible. We are then liberated to *choose* between conflicting values, and to choose the good. That is what freedom in the commonwealth is all about—being responsible and accountable to each other for the sake of love.

On New Year's Day 1990 Václav Havel said,

> Let us teach both ourselves and others that politics ought to be a reflection of the aspiration to contribute to the happiness of the community and not of the need to deceive and pillage the community. Let us teach ourselves and others that politics does not have to be the art of the possible, especially if this means the art of speculating, calculating, intrigues, secret agreements, pragmatic maneuvering, but that it can also be the art of the impossible, that is the art of making both ourselves and the world better. . . . Our worst enemy today is our bad qualities—indifference to public affairs, conceit, ambition, selfishness, the pursuit of personal advancement, and rivalry—and that is the main struggle we are faced with.[18]

This is as true for the United States and Western Europe as it is for Czechoslovakia, Eastern Europe, and the Soviet Union. We live in hope. If the upheavals in Eastern Europe teach us anything, it is that God is full of surprises and that individuals matter and can make a difference.

What will it be like to be ordained in a world in which it is likely that religious belief will become even more personal, less collective, perhaps weaker? Its surrogates (the nation, art, personal relations, and the environment) are likely to flourish. What will it be like to be a minister in a society likely to be more class conscious, and where the gap between the haves and have-nots will widen? Some clergy will fight these trends. Others will give in. Some will be shipwrecked. Others will be very powerful and make a lot of money. I believe that no matter what God reigns and that trying to be faithfully obedient is what is required of us.

The task of the Church and its ministers in the years ahead is to address the spiritual poverty and to help make a family out of strangers. What then do ministers do? They attend to the spiritually impoverished by fulfilling two important functions on behalf of society. They tell stories. They perform rituals. They also act as lightning rods for the issues and anxieties of the day.

CHAPTER SIX

The Minister as Storyteller

Human beings have always told stories, but the importance and power of stories are rarely consciously acknowledged. The widespread popularity of Joseph Campbell's TV series "The Power of Myth" has done a great deal to bring our need of story to consciousness. Ancient myths and stories are about gods and goddesses and the various ways they used to create and order the world. These stories, it is believed, are outward expressions of inner spiritual and psychological events, both for individuals and for communities.

The motif of sacrifice plays through many of these myths and stories; and where there is sacrifice, there is need for a priest, in the ancient sense of the word. Ritual is "repetition" of the acts of the gods who made the world and hold it in being. The priests of old not only helped the community repeat the divine actions but also guarded the stories so that the community could remember its origins.

We all like to tell stories. We all find comfort in repeated acts. There were two stories my wife and I read over and over again to our daughters when they were little: *Mog, the Forgetful Cat* and *The Happy Owls*. I soon grew tired of them and would try for the sake of variety either to skip a page or to change the story ever so slightly. When I did this, there were always screams of protest. The stories had to be repeated in their "pure" form. Our story telling had a ritual quality about it. The stories comforted and reassured our children that all was well, even in a universe that could be dangerous.

I believe I discerned in my children (as I had earlier discovered in myself) a basic sense of ministry that seeks to guard the stories binding us together. I would call this inner sense "priestly." Most of us are largely unconscious of our identity as tellers of tales. Those who do become conscious of it are often in danger of confusing it with a call to be ordained. Our first impulse is to go out and do something, when what we need to do is simply listen to the story as it unfolds inside us. We become conscious of it as we learn to reach out to others.

Words like blessing, sacrifice, delight, thanksgiving, reconciliation, healing, gift, and sacrament are to be found in the stories that bind us together in one community. Underneath these simple words are questions about what sort of world we are building for ourselves and our children. The world we build will depend on the stories we tell.

What About the Great Story—the Bible?

The Bible is a controversial text in modern society. Some people believe that the Bible is "hazardous to your health" if taken literally. It certainly can be dangerous, subversive, and scandalous. Its stories can be used for a variety of purposes, from personal transformation to political revolution. A book that's worth anything is a dangerous object. Storytellers are interested in transformation, and when we enter into a story, something new is in store for us, strange things can happen. That is why books can be dangerous, why people sometimes want to burn them.

I find that I have an ambivalent attitude toward the Bible. On the one hand, it is a book that has nourished and challenged me all my reading life. It is the Word of God. On the other, I have seen people bullied by it. It easily becomes an all-too-human tool.

There are various methods for neutralizing stories, especially the Bible. Both liberals and conservatives in the Church have ways of stifling the text and trivializing and minimizing its scandal. Liberals tend to do it by biblical criticism; conservatives by co-opting the text for very narrow meanings. In both cases the text is used to fortify existing prejudices.

We don't like texts that are ambiguous, contradictory, and ironical. When we are afraid and unsure of ourselves, irony is intolerable. When a story won't fit into our scheme of things, it is offensive not only to the congregation but to the preacher, the storyteller.[1]

On one level the Bible is utterly useless, in spite of what some people think. It doesn't tell us about abortion, about the current political situation, about the death penalty. It addresses an audience other than us (we are not with Moses on the Plains of Moab or in Rome with Mark or on Patmos with John). Yet it speaks to us across the centuries. We are invited to enter into another world. We are invited to imagine another world, with different rules, a different joy, a different obedience. You don't have to like it or agree with it or defend it. Let it speak! Watch and listen. The text will tell us something we did not know. We go to the text "with awed anticipation, knowing we are unlikely to hear a voice addressing us we have never heard before, saying to us what we have never heard before."

No One Can Exist Without a Text

Walter Brueggemann rightly insists that "we are essentially textual creatures." There are no textless people. Everyone has a text, known or unknown. It may be an actual text or a very personal one, like "My dad always said . . . " "My mother always told me . . . " Or it may be a story constructed out of an experience of happiness or hurt. Old happenings become texts for us. Most of them are unrecognized and uncriticized and are therefore very powerful. We live in and through the stories we have been told. One way to understand why people find some form of psychotherapy useful at certain times in their lives is that, at its best, it brings "to speech the hidden texts and invisible loyalties out of which we live." As Brueggemann notes, "The psychotherapeutic notion that we are scripted people is so utterly, utterly Jewish. Jews order life around script, not around ideas. In Jewish epistemology, ideas are only spin-offs from texts, but life consists in our texts, in studying, receiving, serving, criticizing, and answering our texts. What has happened in modernity is that we have abandoned our text."[2]

What happens when we abandon our stories? Brueggemann points out that we become quarrelsome. We fight over ideas instead of jointly listening to the playful themes of stories. Without stories we have no arena where we can adjudicate our conflicts in a creative way. A story gives us room.

When the Church scuttles its own sacred text, other texts intrude, because we cannot live for very long without one. "So now we have on our hands in the church alien texts that sound authoritative, texts of secular humanism, texts of free market advocacy, texts of moral absolutism, texts of individualism, all of which are idolatrous texts that are pitiful when contrasted with the dense, rich playfulness of our text."[3]

The clergy are not the only tellers of tales and guardians of texts, but they are key people in the battle over texts in our culture. It cannot be said often enough: Stories, books, and texts are dangerous, because they have the power to create communities, communities often at war with each other.

Brueggemann makes an implicit demand on the ordained. Ministers must be able to stand in two places at once with regard to the Bible. They must be able to hold a critical distance and at the same time be willing to plunge into its deep and impenetrable waters. He asks us to be clear about the distinction between our studying the text and living the story. "The text implies that I can be and must be someone other than I assumed myself to be prior to hearing. If the text cannot create a different community of pain and obedience, nothing can, certainly not our scholastic certitude, certainly not our historical criticism, certainly not our best theology."[4]

The minister, as storyteller, invites people into a threatening place of radical reinterpretation of their lives and their world. The Bible attacks "the closed orthodoxies of economics, politics, psychology, theology, or morality." *This* text is not another little closed orthodoxy. "It is a protest against all closed orthodoxies, left, right and center. It is the voice of holy freedom that shatters all closedness for the news; it is the voice of free holiness that refuses to let us be where we are on our own terms."[5]

The stories ministers have to tell are as upsetting to the tellers as to the hearers. The text is supposed to upset us, by playing on our imagination and undermining and destabilizing our tidy view of the world. The preacher knows how destructive certitude can be. Ministers are ordained to bring people to threshold experiences where they can understand life afresh.

When and where are these experiences to be found? Brueggemann sees the threshold of the new in three places: in art, therapy, and texts. I would add worship, which in a sense encompasses all three. Our world constantly needs repatterning and reordering. Things happen to us when we tell stories and share bread.

The Function of Stories:
To Nurture a Community of Trust

Three ideas, closely associated with ministry, come into play when we tell important stories about our origin and our destiny: community, communion, and trust. Without basic trust, the world is not fit to live in. Unless we can learn to give and keep our word to each other, there is no hope for a truly human and humanizing community. How can we get the conversation going about building a community of trust? Communities need a common fund of stories to bind them together. If we want to find those people who are functioning as "ministers" (good or bad) in our society, all we have to do is look for those who guard and pass on the stories.

E. D. Hirsch, Jr., understood the need for a common narrative when he put together his *Cultural Literacy,* in which he lists all the information we need to know to tell the story of our culture.[6] In order for a society to have a common story, its citizens need to learn a certain amount of information. Unless children learn and absorb a lot of data, the story of their people will be unintelligible to them. In our culture there is, of course, more than one version of the story. There are even rival stories or gospels.

Richard Rorty, a professor at the University of Virginia, has his own version of the story and is a "priest" of the liberal left. He cannot live without texts. He imagines an updated John Dewey

wanting the children to come to think of themselves as proud and loyal citizens of a country that, slowly and painfully, threw off a foreign yoke, freed its slaves, enfranchised its women, restrained its robber barons and licensed its trade unions, liberalized its religious practices and broadened its religious and moral tolerance, and built colleges in which 50 per cent of its population could enroll—a country that numbered Ralph Waldo Emerson, Eugene V. Debs, Susan B. Anthony and James Baldwin among its citizens.[7]

Rorty's is one version of the story, and he tells it well. His gospel is shared by many Americans. In many ways it is in tune with some versions of the Christian gospel. The trouble is that the ordained are stuck with words that many have long since been rejected, words like *God, Church,* and *minister.* Even those who insist that we ought to dispense with such words get caught in inventing another vocabulary that looks suspiciously like the old one.

The Problem of Religious Language

What words should we use and what stories should we tell about "this unnamed and unsignposted expanse of our consciousness"?[8] We are in a bind with regard to words. Some still fear or despise religion because its stories hurt as well as heal. The Bible, the great collection of stories of the Christian community, has been so abused that for some people it is virtually a lost book. The contemporary minister as the bearer of the word, the teller of tales, often and unfairly has to bear the blame for the damage done to souls in the Bible's name.

In our culture the words of religion are tired and stale. They are overused, and there is no word more stale and tired than the word *God.* Religious stories are discredited in the United States because they have been abused.

How does "God" get lost? When God-talk gets polluted, when we insist on treating "God" as an idea, as either a good or a bad one, humanity is worse off. For some, the sooner we scrap this idea and realize that our stories are just stories the better. It is thought that "religion" tends to distract us from the real business of looking after this world by directing our attention to another and unreal one. If the myths tells us anything, they remind us that there *is* another world, but it's the same as this one![9] The notion persists, however, that we shall be more authentically human when we get rid of religious language. As Nicholas Lash points out, "If God is an idea, then the dispute between theism and atheism is merely a dispute as to whether this idea is a useful or a harmful fiction."[10]

Lash poses the question of dispensing with this kind of theism and, of course, the atheisms that rely on it. We might, after jettisoning a merely "useful" God, look at revising and recovering our view of humanity in the light of the recurring stories that will not die or be co-opted

78

for mere utilitarian reasons. The suggestion is that if we do, the true and living God may appear.

The implications for the ordained ministry are staggering. We would cease to be slaves to ideology and learn to be free souls.[11] We might realize that "atheism is a crutch for those who cannot bear the reality of God."[12] Atheism "is the condition of those who . . . are so locked into narcissistic self-absorption as to be cut off from relationship with God."[13]

The minister is the storyteller, the bearer of the Word. The function of story telling is to get us out of this narcissistic bind. And surely our narcissism is our common and great enemy. That is the root of our so-called atheism. In the first instance belief in God is a way of talking about our being rescued from our loneliness by means of the miracle of love.

The Attraction of False Stories

Some citizens wish to designate the United States a Christian nation. This springs from a peculiarly distorted version of the Christian story. Some people in the United States think that being Christian and standing up for "family values" means being racist and anti-Semitic. No wonder some secular humanists treat religion with indifference or contempt. We would be better off without such stories.

This raises the question of the nature of Christian narrative and its relationship to society. In what sense can a nation be said to be Christian, Jewish, Muslim, Buddhist, or secular? How would we tell a common and inclusive story that honored yet transcended our differences?

The confusion about religion in the West is made all the more apparent by the exhibition of unrestrained fanaticism on the part of Christian, Islamic, and Jewish fundamentalists. The post-Christian nations are not clear about their beliefs or values. They lack a coherent story. We are so liberal and plural that we fail to appreciate the fact that other peoples live from a deep level of longing that comes out in what are to us bizarre beliefs and "irrational" acts. We "believe" in the market-place, the laws of "common sense"—things that bear little or no relation to the limitless mystery to which or to whom we are oriented and related.

The "priests" of our consumerist creed are the celebrants of an economically determined world characterized by short-term and short-sighted desires for gratification. We have no reason to keep our word for long because we have a short-term view of things. Our stories get shorter and shorter and are narcissistically concerned with personal safety and success.

But we underestimate the importance of long-running religious stories. They are the source of personal identity, social integration, and overarching vision. We need someone or something to tell us who we are, how we are to be with each other, and where we are going. We need to be grounded in shared beliefs. We need a common story, and we need people with the memory to go on telling it. We need a community we can trust. We need to minister to one another.

Pluralism and Confusion
Are Built into Our Story

We come by our religious confusion honestly. After all, America was founded by people who had a chip on their shoulder about religion, and with good cause. Many came clutching the Bible, the Word. In its pages they thought they found clear principles for governing ourselves and our society. For our forebears, religion was not a hobby or a trivial pursuit. The Puritans of New England had been treated with a heavy hand in the old country, and they were equally if not more heavy-handed with their fellow citizens in their new homeland. "They fined, whipped, jailed, cropped, maimed and hanged in an effort to maintain a pure social order and to erect a *true* Church of Christ"![14] Cotton Mather in Massachussetts saw Rhode Island as the latrine of New England because that tiny and despised colony gave safe harbor to "Antinomians, Familists, Anabaptists, Antisabbatarians, Arminians, Socinians, Quakers, Ranters—everything in the world except Roman Catholics and real Christians." Our forebears were scandalized by diversity.

No wonder Thomas Paine responded, "The most detestable wickedness, the most horrid cruelties, and the greatest miseries that have afflicted the human race, have had their origin in this thing called revelation, or revealed religion." Wouldn't it be better to leave our longings to silence? How awful to tell a story about them and then force others to accept the story as dogma. Yet this is what generations of ordained ministers thought was their vocation.

We have the choice of either being dangerously focused or fatuously vague about words like *God, Church,* and *minister.* I am willing to give them up if someone will come up with a way of addressing our need for a community of trust in the context of a world understood as sacred. In 1890 the Supreme Court spoke of Americans as a Christian Nation, a Christian People. In 1952 the Court was content to call Americans a religious people whose institutions presuppose a Supreme Being. It is prudent to be as vague as possible!

It is neither possible nor desirable to separate entirely the essence of religion from its cultural manifestations. We do need, however, to do a little sorting out. We have various forms of social and cultural religiosity. In much of the South, everyone is Baptist, even the atheists, because it is a Baptist culture. New England Congregationalism colors everything there. People outside of California think of Californians as a tribe of laid-back hedonists. I was brought up to make little or no distinction between a Christian and English gentleman. Recently I came across what I can only describe as Methodist Buddhism in Hawaii. I visited a temple modeled on a Methodist chapel. The Buddhist bishop acknowledged the sect's debt to American Protestantism when he knowingly and with a smile summed up Buddhism in the phrase "Buddha loves me, this I know, for the *gathas* tell me so." One of the hymns written by a former Anglican priest went like this:

> Ever onward, Ever upward,
> Gently held by Love's embrace
> Till we reach Nirvana's summit
> And behold Truth face to face.

I am not put off by this. I think it is part of the movement of the Spirit to form us into one people. In practice those who want to call America a Christian Nation cannot stand the idea of a Great Story that insists that we are one human family. They tend not only to be racist and anti-Semitic but sexist and separatist as well. It is a form of Christian story telling that is exclusive, individualistic, and coercive. The list of those of us who are definitely not included in this narrow "Christian" commonwealth is impressive. That kind of story telling produces an ordained ministry to match.

What is the alternative? The secular solutions offer no hope. As we have seen, modernity has been defined as the situation where nothing is sacred. And that in the end is intolerable. We need to live in a sacred space. We need those among us who are willing to utter the sacred words. The sad thing about the furor over Salman Rushdie's novel *The Satanic Verses* was not so much the fanatical protests it occasioned but the way it illustrated our indifference to the holy. Blasphemy is obsolete. The answer lies not in the revival of blasphemy laws, of course, but in the recovery of the world as sacred space.

"Tell Them What They Want to Hear!"

The trouble is that the sacred words themselves have been debased to serve base interests. Sociologist Peter Berger demonstrates how "religious symbols are employed to legitimate class interests and class culture."[15] Each class calls in the clergy to bless its troops. Priests and ministers prostitute their profession in the interests of short-term gain. Berger is reacting against a belligerent and excommunicating "liberalism" that has overtaken the mainline churches—excommunicating because we tend to anathematize those who don't agree with us. The prophetic mission of the Church is often tied to specific political agendas. This is deadly. When we identify with a particular program, we in effect excommunicate those who disagree with us.

We are good at spotting the ways we exclude with regard to race and gender but not so good when it comes to political opinions. The new Christian Right, for example, is a crusade to change American society with highly specific programs, about which there is no shadow of doubt. The same can be said of some left-wing Christians. In the religious world we suffer from the disease of God-is-on-our-sidism. Peter Berger points this out with relish. "God is *for* tuition tax credits; God is against them. God is for the MX missile; God is against it. God is pro-life; God is pro-choice." We subscribe to rival orthodoxies. We tell the stories to suit our clientele. There are no ambiguities, no areas of uncertainty. There is no community of trust, no saving word binding us together, no God worth believing in, no tale to tell.

A substantial percentage of the population wants to believe in someone or something, but they don't want to belong to an organization, still less to a denomination. They want a do-it-yourself religion. To be one's own minister, telling one's own private story in one's own private religion, fits right in with those who want to believe but don't want to belong.

The conversation into which Christianity invites us is not easy. It is like learning a new language and is not immediately accessible. The question is, How far are we willing to work, to think? To be an American or an Englishman means knowing something of your nation's story. There are dates and events, people and places to remember. We used to be able to say, "Every schoolchild knows . . . " Now we are not so sure what they know. Christians are supposed to know the story of Israel and of Jesus well enough to interpret and experience themselves and their world in its terms.[16] That involves work.

Christianity (like being English or American) is a form of life that has to be learned and practiced. The trouble is that churches have become purveyors of package deals. Clergy sell a story rather than tell one. They do not draw people into a community of shared meanings. The package deal tends to be a subtle or crass (depending on the denomination or form of the religion) way of reinforcing one's own narcissistic agenda.

Elmer F. Suderman in *The Smell of Perfumed Assemblies* writes about his congregation:

> Baptized in the smell
> of classic Chanel
> I promote their nod
> to a jaunty God
> Who, they are sure,
> is a sparkling gem
> superbly right for them.
> There they go
> my in-crowd
> my soft-skin crowd,
> elegant, swellegant
> natty, delectable,
> suave, cool, adorable
> DAMNED
>
> Yes damned. Saved by grace perhaps. Certainly not helped by my cowardly
> silence.[17]

This devastating comment is all the more unnerving for those of us who are ordained. What kind of vocation is it to be expected to act as spiritual sycophants to people self-absorbed in private spiritual journeys, who are interested only in short stories about themselves?

The consumerist approach to spirituality makes belief in God very difficult because the word *God* is often merely a buzzword for good feelings about oneself and bad feelings about the people we don't like. "God" is part of the paraphernalia of the religion industry. Ministers are in the business of market research, looking for better ways to package and sell "God" rather than tell a story. No wonder many of the ordained fall apart, take to drink, try to find solace in sex, or lapse into low-grade depression.

I see no point in our going on talking about God unless God somehow addresses us. How do we get the conversation going when religion and religious experience seems to be, for many, either a pastime or a narcotic, a thing to dull the pain of everyday existence? I ask myself, "What is it that continually causes me to mistrust?" This question strikes at the heart of my priesthood. The issue for me is one of trust and fidelity. Is there anything or anyone in whom I can have confidence?

As I grow older, I am overcoming my embarrassment at the company I have to keep because I believe in God. Is this because, for me, time is running out? Or is it because I am seeing things more clearly? Raising the question of and even believing in God are at least tolerated nowadays in intellectual circles. To be sure, some still assume that raising the question of God is a sign of an attempt to escape from or to evade the implications of the here and now. Religion, seen as pure escapism, is regarded as something "too childish to be discussed seriously."[18] Still, I would guess that many intellectuals nowadays are more willing at least to entertain the idea of God than they were twenty years ago. This is encouraging, because there is no hope of building a community of trust if one side thinks the other is a bunch of idiots. Questions of trust can now be looked at in a way that gives hope for the development of a community out of strangers.

People on both sides of the God question used to embarrass me. On one side were secular humanists and other "godless atheists," on the other were those who had God in their pocket, the fundamentalists and the sectarians. The complaisant god of accommodating liberalism died on me some years ago. In my own church there is a growing split between liberals of the trendy sort and conservatives who have many of the right words but seem to know little of the music. I am a liberal from an older tradition. I miss our being able to confront one another with civility and compassion on issues that excite and concern us.

Recovering the Lost Art of Conversation

In order for a common story or word to appear, we need to revive the lost art of conversation. We don't know how to use words to heal and make new. This is a priestly art. We don't know how to "entertain" an idea—simply to let it sit there while we think about it, without any pressure to take it home to live with us. All that is required is that we enter into conversation for the cycle of blessing to be revived. Martin Buber wrote, "I have no teaching, but carry on a conversation. . . . In the beginning was the relation."[19] Buber knew that the first human being was nature's priest. Adam existed only in relation to God. He was defined by his basic orientation to mystery. It is because of this basic orientation that I am not interested in talking about God to anyone until we have decided how we are going to relate to each other and how we are to behave in the world.

All the great religious stories are about the relationship or covenant with God and with one another. This motif is central to our story. In short, before we can talk about God, I need to be able to trust you. I want to be assured that you have heard the call to be available, to be compassionate. I want to be in the company of someone who knows enough of the Great Stories and who is capable of both sacrifice and delight, someone who wants to create a circle of mutual blessing. I want to be in a conversation about these Great Stories. In the first instance, I don't care what the other person believes. Our beliefs and our premature rush into hermeneutics (our need to interpret an idea before we have entertained it) cause us to be hopelessly estranged from each other. When we rush to define the world before we actually take a look at it, we kill the conversation.

A friend of mine translates the first verses of Saint John's Gospel in this way: "In the beginning was the Conversation. The conversation was not only with God, the conversation was God. And nothing that has happened or will happen happens outside that conversation. Then in John's own time, the conversation sounded in our flesh and not only did we hear it—we saw it! Saw it in all its splendor, new as it always will be in the womb of the Father."[20]

I wonder what would happen if we treated dogmas as the means by which the tradition initiates a conversation as a prelude to story telling? Instead, people see them as great horse-pills to swallow. The liberal wants to update them, the conservative to swallow them as they are. I want to be in conversation with them and tell stories about them. By that I don't mean an armchair chat over a beer. I mean something of what Franz Kafka meant when he wrote about the effect books should have on us:

> If the book we are reading does not wake us as with a fist hammering on the skull, why then do we read it? So that it should make us happy? Good God, we would also be happy if we had no books, and such books as make us happy we could, if need be, write ourselves. But what we must have are those books [dogmas] which come upon us like ill-fortune, and distress us deeply, like the death of one we love better than ourselves, like suicide. A book must be an ice-axe to break the sea frozen inside us.[21]

Imagine the mighty stories of the great faiths of the world as ice-axes to break the sea frozen inside us to liberate us into a community of trust! Imagine that they are love letters from God that initiate a conversation and teach us how to love each other. These love letters teach me how to give and keep my word. Dogma, as a tool, teaches me how to look at you, how to read you, how to listen to and speak to you, because you too are a story. When I try to read you, to understand what you are about, the doctrines of the Church come upon me like an ice-axe to break the sea frozen inside me. Dogma is a kind of spiritual sledgehammer to set free the depths within us.

Talk about God (dogma) initiates a conversation that can lead anywhere. The job of the minister as storyteller is to initiate and enable the conversation by telling a version of the story that will build a community of trust. It is to help each of us become as good as his or her word. Our word needs to find its meaning and value in the light of the Word that some call God.

Singing the Song That Binds Us Together

If dogma is an ice-axe, then how can we describe its application? I searched for a story that reflected (at least not directly) neither the received Christian versions nor the secularized liberal versions. Bruce Chatwin provided the example of an Australian aborigine in his novel *The Songlines*.[22] Australian aboriginal myths are alien to both popular Christian stories and their secular counterparts yet speak across cultural lines about how a community of trust is maintained by stories, dreams, and songs. Chatwin's novel is about the way the world is held together by songlines or dreaming-tracks. "Aboriginal Creation myths tell of legendary totemic beings who wandered over the continent in the Dreamtime, singing out the name of everything that crossed their path—birds, animals, plants, rocks, water-holes—and so singing the world into existence." A character in the book, Arkady, explains

> how each Ancestor, while travelling through the country, was thought to have scattered a trail of words and musical notes along the line of his footprints, and how these Dreaming-tracks lay over the land as 'ways' of communication between the most far-flung tribes. 'A song,' he said, 'was both map and direction-finder. Providing you knew the song, you could always find your way across country. . . . In theory, at least, the whole of Australia could be read as a musical score.[23]

"To them, the whole of bloody Australia is sacred," comments the Westerner. We might add, "To us, the whole of the bloody world is sacred." The sacredness of the world is a meeting place for many stories. And music provides a place where many people (who adhere to rival ideologies) can meet.

Each child, according to the myth, is born with a fragment of the Song. The suggestion is that if we all were in touch with the music we were born with, we would not only be bound together in one community but we would be free to move about as we please because we would know our way about. We would have at our fingertips the musical map, the songlines, crisscrossing our history and experience. Each generation needs to sing and tell the stories to keep the lines deep and clear. This is a powerful metaphor for ministry.

Stories for People on the Move

It seems to me that much of Western theology has been all lyrics and no music with regard to the sacredness of creation. Our pain has to do with the fact that the earth is where we belong and yet we are not completely at home here. That is why stories of journeying, pilgrimage, and even simple walking are important. The minister (in this case the novelist) is the guardian of these stories. The call to "walk about" speaks to our not being able to get to the bottom of them.

Chatwin knows about this uneasiness and incorporates it into his story. He acknowledges his debt to Osip Mandelstam's *Journey to Armenia* and *Conversations About Dante*. Chatwin writes, "As a Jew, [Mandelstam] understands restlessness—at one point he speaks about 'our fantastic homelessness.'" Mandelstam loved the poet Dante because "the *Inferno* and especially the *Purgatorio* glorify the human gait, the measure and rhythm of walking, the foot and its shape." We need to walk more if we are to dare to talk about God. It is sorted out by walking—*Solvitur ambulando,* exclaimed Saint Augustine. Ministers need to see themselves as both pilgrims on the move and as shrine guardians (a thing not to be despised), places where stories are told and retold.

Søren Kierkegaard wrote (in a letter in 1847): "Above all do not lose your desire to walk: every day I walk myself into a state of well-being and walk away from every illness; I have walked myself into my best thoughts, and I know of no thought so burdensome that one cannot walk away from it." And note the Buddha's last command to his disciples, "Walk on!" The aboriginal wisdom of the walkabout is found in many traditions. It is a way of establishing patterns of connection and communion by means of movement and story telling. We too need to get moving to make the dreaming-tracks and the songlines that hold our world together. The minister is a storyteller, a dreamer, a singer.

We Are One Communion

There are fragments of this in my own Anglican (Episcopal) tradition. The language and the cultural setting is very different from those of the aborigine myth but it is clear that in my tradition we understand ourselves as one communion—"sociable parts united into one body," as the sixteenth-century theologian Richard Hooker put it.

It is also clear that stories need to be told in more than one way. It is not sufficient to read them out of a book. They have to be celebrated, acted out so that the reality of which they speak can actually happen. Ritual and liturgy are important for bringing the world into existence in this aboriginal sense. We rightly expect ministers to perform rituals and celebrate liturgies. Rituals create communities of trust. They do it by dramatizing a story that reminds us of our past and brings that past into the present in such a way that we use it to project ourselves into the future with confidence.

Fidelity is required if the story is to ring true. That is why we have to be in constant conversation with it and about it. It isn't a dead story. It is a living one, and for it to be truly alive, we must be free to question it, to collide with it, to argue over its true meaning, and to struggle with others about where it is leading us. To do this I must be able to trust you and you to trust me. It is the key by which our passion and concern for each other draws us into the conversation about God's Passion and compassion.

Fidelity to Each Other
Means Sacrifice

One of the tough assignments of the minister is to combat the mistaken idea that people are independent of one another and that social relations are accidental or a necessary evil. Your fate is my business and mine is yours. But if reality truly is what the aboriginal myth claims— genuinely sacred—then true life for the self involves commitment to others in ways that will require acts of both sacrifice and delight. The Great Story insists that the group has more claims on us than we would like. Something has to be sacrificed for a community of trust to be born. David Smith writes, "A life of fidelity, in other words, is a life of *increased* vulnerability to suffering that comes from identifying oneself with other frail and broken persons. The enlarged sense of self and rooting in God's love mean this suffering is borne in hope." Here, for me, the story gets specifically Christian, because those of us who know this drama cannot help but think of Jesus in Gethsemane. Jesus is the revelation of "power committing itself to others and being crucified into the bargain" for the sake of making a community out of strangers and false friends.[24] This is the context of ministry.

It should be clear by now that all I can offer are the bits and pieces of an agenda for a possible conversation, the fragments of a musical score, a few suggestions of a way for us to stumble into fulfilling our ministry.

My concern is the relationship of dogma, doctrine, and believing to the formation of a community that is on the move.

As a minister, I make one important assumption, that I believe that I have more in common with anyone with whom I find myself on the road than anything that could possibly divide us. My first test of orthodoxy has to do with mutual trust: "If you had the chance, would you do me in?"

I tried that on an orthodox rabbi friend recently and he replied, with a twinkle in his eye, "That depends!" I think he had Adolf Hitler in mind. The rabbi reminded me that human beings can be dangerous and predatory animals who easily lose their way. What do we do when others hurt and disappoint us? There's something in me that wants to tell a story. The rabbis were and are great storytellers. A father complained once to the great Baal Shem Tov that his son had forsaken God. "What, Rabbi, shall I do?" "Love him more than ever" was the reply.

Being Is Communion; Reality Is Community

What we have discovered so far about the minister as the guardian of the narrative can be expressed in two aphorisms: being is communion and reality is community. This is what the songlines teach us. This is what is revealed in the New Testament. It is echoed in the teachings of Buddha and of Islam. We find it in the myth making of secular humanists and so-called nonbelievers.

In his book *Easter in Ordinary* Nicholas Lash revives Immanuel Kant's four basic questions: What can I know? What ought I to do? What may I hope? and What is man? Kant raised the last question of human identity but did not answer it. I would like to answer Kant's last question by suggesting that the word *blessing* is the key. Lash asks, "What if the answer is 'nothing'!" Perhaps "there is no reliable knowledge, no clear lines of duty, and . . . all hope is illusory. . . . So we cling to such comfort as we can." We rely on our wealth (we love rags-to-riches stories) and on such structure as we have managed to build (we love the secular myths about the "superiority" of our way of life). If we cannot attempt to answer the first three questions, then the fourth is pointless. It doesn't even arise. If the question of the human cannot be raised in any reliable way, then neither can the question of God, "because the holy mystery that is God only appears in human words and in human relationships."[25]

But I find the reverse is also true. If it is pointless to talk about God when we can't even talk about the human, it seems to me that we cannot help stumbling into and over the word *God* when we try to talk about what it might mean to be human. Our myths and stories cannot do without certain key words and ideas. Human relatedness of any meaning appears only when the relationship of God is seen as possible. Words like *community* and even *communion* keep slipping in.

Theology is then practiced under another name. It is called philosophy, politics, or literary criticism. The followers of these disciplines tell stories, guard particular orthodoxies, and preach a gospel. Each has its own priesthood and hierarchy, because all of us are looking for a community of trust.

True Knowledge Is What I Can Trust

Lash suggests that questions of epistemology (what and how can we know) are better construed as questions concerning the trustworthiness of people and the reliability of things.[26] To recover trust we must be more respectful of tradition and be committed to the recovery of the public world where conversation and story telling are possible. Why? Because commitment to the truth is a be*troth*ing. It binds and brings us into relationship. Public story telling is very difficult in a society that is understandably paranoid about the separation of Church and State. Stories, particularly religious ones, must be left to the private sector. This severely hampers public education. It is hard to get under the skin of things without the freedom to tell Great Stories. Perhaps that's why education is more concerned with the passing on of information than with the imparting of wisdom. My really knowing something or someone, as opposed to knowing about, "requires not simply skills of alertness and intelligence, but also some sort of sympathy and the incurring of the risks of friendship."[27] Imagine that! My knowing is contingent on my ability to risk friendship. We come back to my wanting to learn how to give and keep my word, which is the same as "plighting my troth." We are back to the theme of communion and community. When we begin to trust each other, a new world opens up. The entry to this other world—the God-world—is through the door of story telling, compassion, and friendship.

In other words, I cannot bring up the question of God in any meaningful way without telling the story about the formation of a trustworthy and reliable community. I want not so much a shelter from the storm as a community where everyone has a place, and not just any place but an honored one. There's no point in having a little "god" just for me. I don't want to be part of a priesthood of one. Lash points out that an inclusive community "is a necessary condition to the possibility of prayer, of address to God, of living in his presence."[28] Thus, already I have made a condition of the conversation—or Word—about God. Whatever the word *God* means, it must imply a story about an inclusive community. Whatever ministry is, it must be concerned with story telling and communion.

There are several reasons why the question of God and the question of community go together, not least because of the way I experience myself as open and vulnerable when I reject the illusion of self-sufficiency. The openness of our "nature" makes us vulnerable. Human beings don't just happen. In one sense we have to decide to be human, and that decision has to be made every waking moment.

This component to being human, which is "beyond biology," pushes us into God-talk, story telling, and, hence, ministry. "The question of God" and "the question of the human" are mutually dependent. The meeting place for these two questions is in our ministry, in knowing we are blessed and are called to bless in return.

CHAPTER SEVEN

The Minister as Artist

As storytellers, ministers are called to be artists of the imagination, poets of the spiritual life. Art is an important metaphor for ministry, because art has to do with the way we imagine the world. Ministers deal in images. Art is also inherently dangerous and destabilizing. Ministers present a view of the world that can be radically upsetting. A work of art opens one up to wonder and leaves one wondering.

The stories we tell are works of art, and the infuriating thing about a work of art is that it doesn't mean any *one* thing. There are always levels of meaning, some of them contradictory. Our stories, then, are works of art and therefore resist easy and shallow interpretation. The meanings are always easily accessible because a great piece of art both invites and resists interpretation. This is what makes art "godly" and ministers artists.

Christian faith is a work of art. It too does not lend itself to easy interpretation. It is a pilgrimage, a journey into mystery. Like a great piece of music, serious faith leaves deep questions disturbingly open. The architecture of the great cathedrals is an attempt to work some magic on us, to cast a spell, to bring us into contact with the story at a deeper level. I'm not referring to "magic" in its modern trivialized and manipulative sense. I mean, rather, the power (through art) to bring to light that other world which interpenetrates the ordinary world we only sleepily experience.

The problems with regard to art and artists are analogous to religion and the ordained. Art has to be both authentic and accessible. Religion has to be demanding and understandable. How do we maintain a balance between elitism and a lowest-common-denominator kind of art or religion? How is the story lived out in the world? Is there "a poetry of everyday life"? I think there is.

In my tradition (and in many others), the clergy are not only storytellers but also bread-breakers—bearers of sacraments that feed and heal. The sacraments (particularly baptism and the eucharist) are the story in action. They are food for pilgrims as they try to find their way through the labyrinth of human experience. The two great maps for Christians are the Bible and the sacraments. The ordained are among those called to read these maps and to help others through the labyrinth.

The Golden String

The title of Father Bede Griffiths's autobiography, *The Golden String,* is taken from a line in a William Blake poem:

> I give you the end of a golden string:
> Only wind it into a ball,
> It will lead you in at heaven's gate,
> Built in Jerusalem's Wall.

Father Griffiths comments, "To follow up the vision which we have seen, to keep it in mind when we are thrown back again on the world, to live in its light and shape our lives by its law, is to wind the string into a ball, and find our way out of the labyrinth of life."[1] Inscribed on the ground outside the temple at the Saccidananda Ashram in India are these words in English: "Every temple built outside us is the blueprint of the destiny everyone has to reach within."[2] In the language we have been using, ministry (the life characterized by sacrifice and delight) is our destiny, and every church and temple are blueprints of the journey of discovery. Ministers are artists whose lives are spent with the blueprint of stories and bread breaking.

The vision of the sacred is a golden string that leads us in the path of sacrifice and transformation, by means of story telling and bread breaking. It is the path of the poet, and ministers are poets of the spiritual path. The stories we tell make sure that nothing is left out of the process, because that which is suppressed is incapable of transformation. The terrible vision of the Nazi death camps is as much a part of human experience as is the vision of communion and community in heaven. We need a golden string to lead us through the labyrinth of conflicting visions. We need stories, myths, and poems to pull us through. We need artists, poets, and ministers to act as guides and interpreters.

Ministers of the Imagination

The ordained are ministers of the Imagination. A poem by a friend of mine speaks to this ministry of images. To be a minister is to be an interpreter, a translator. The poem is about time, our dramatic passage through it, and the way myth and history are intertwined in our individual and collective experiences. Underneath is the glorious assumption that God is the poet (maker) of our lives. We are products of the divine imagination. The last two lines are particularly important.

> Once upon a time there was no time
> Before the creation, the alpha,
> After the last day, the omega
> Of this great world, now and here
> Made present to us at the quick
> And the turn of the new year.
> At the turn of the new Adam
> Turned up again out of hell,
> Rolling away the stone
> For the old Adam as well.
> At the quick from the straw
> The new man cried. His mother
> Laid him down in a manger,
> To be a light to lighten our dark
> And ride the flood as in the ark;
> For this mythology is true
> In the beginning and in you.[3]

To follow the impulse of the creative imagination is to be on a spiritual path. You cannot help yourself. "For this mythology is true / In the beginning and in you." Finding your "myth" and celebrating its origin in and connection with the Great Myth or Love Story of Creation and Re-Creation is the purpose of life.

We live in a time of impoverished imagination. We cannot live without its energy and power. It is the faculty by which we look into the reality of things or, better, the faculty by which the reality of things look into us.

Ministry as Art:
The Work of the Creative Imagination

Creativity is both dangerous and inevitable for human beings: dangerous because it is the way human beings assume the prerogative of God; inevitable because these same beings (so the myth runs) are made after the image of this God. To create is to be godlike and to be human is to be godlike. Human beings cannot help but live from their creative imaginations. Insofar as we are truly human, we are all poets and priests. We are all, like Hermes, intermediaries between spirit and matter. We all make things. We all sacrifice them to some god or other. We are also manufacturers of shoddy goods, spiritual and intellectual as well as physical.

Eric Gill, a complex and perverse artist, in a famous aphorism stated that "All art is propaganda." That is why it is dangerous. A work of art is a word made flesh, an incarnation. We have to be careful about what we want to enflesh. That is why I tend to give only two cheers for the imagination. I hold one cheer back because of the obvious and unacknowledged dangers in its undisciplined and unrefined use. The imagination tends "to fornicate promiscuously with her own images," to use W. H. Auden's phrase. In other words, we tend to fall in love with our own creativity, our own cleverness. We get intoxicated by our own imagined genius. We forget that we have to be in the service of someone or something. We have to be someone's or something's "minister" or "priest."

We love the image rather than the truth to which it points. The word for this perversion is *idolatry*. That is why artists are often accused of trivializing evil and idealizing neurosis. Yet we are all artists one way or another, even if only the clumsy artisans of our own lives. Our imaginative constructions are all very fragile. As we have seen, we cannot stand the powerlessness of which this fragility is but one manifestation. Primo Levi points out that the one point that all of Hitler's biographers can agree on is his flight from reality that marked his last years. "He had forbidden and denied his subjects any access to truth, contaminating their morality and their memory. . . . His collapse was not only a salvation for mankind but also a demonstration of the price to be paid when one dismembers the truth."[4] The maniac dismembers. The artist remembers. Hitler's manipulation of memory destroyed the will to make decisions. When the ability to decide is amputated, we are not responsible and cannot therefore be punished.[5] With such insidious strategies, we try to circumvent the fragility to which our powerlessness introduces us. The result? Dismemberment. The paradox? It isn't until we, like bread, are broken and given away (dismembered) that true communion is celebrated.

Our Awesome Fragility

Ministers are called to be in touch with a certain kind of fragility, a fragility that has to do with the unfinishedness of human existence. The key word here is one we have encountered before: *transcendence*. We are straining toward something beyond us. All our efforts are approximations. The artist in us is never satisfied, still less is he or she self-satisfied. Occasionally we see this "something" with startling clarity. Most of the time we stumble around in the dark. We improvise all the time. It's called living!

What most of us don't know or don't want to know is that we live simultaneously in two different worlds: an inner and an outer. We need to learn to live in and with both if we are not to go mad.

The poet sees something I am afraid to see or cannot see and enables me to look; and thus I in my turn am invited to become a poet, to become a minister or priest. I do this by becoming *responsible* (by *responding*) to the vision. And in looking with fear, awe, or delight (depending on the object of my gaze), I am opened up to new possibilities and new responsibilities. I become a little less manipulable by the Hitlers of the world. I become more clearly God's minister.

We are all poets or makers, even if what we make of things doesn't appear to amount to much. Even the very least of what I am is considerable. I am a cocreator with God of my own person. Marcel Proust wrote: "Every reader is, while he is reading, the reader of his own self. The writer's work is merely a kind of optical instrument, which he offers to the reader to enable him to discern what, without the book, he would perhaps never have perceived for himself." I think that is why I read so much—I am looking for clues to my identity, for signs of my true self, for the golden string. The poet or novelist provides me with images of self-recognition, images I need if I am to interpret myself and find my way out of the labyrinth of false enchantments.

We are all subject to the assault of images, images that make us or mar us. The question is how can the imagination be both free and regulated? How can it be wild without being destructive? How do you tell the difference between creative imagination and restrictive fantasy? We need an overarching set of regulating images that point to values like communion and compassion.

The Need for a Certain Kind of Folly

Artists go "mad" and suffer deeply for our sake, and we should be prepared to look out for and after them when they go mad. As God's fools, ministers should respect the fool and the idiot in our midst. Traditionally the king in his court needed the former, and every village had the latter. The fool, the idiot, and the minister serve a vital function in expanding our horizons and exploding the confines of what we call human and define as natural.

The artist in this sense is almost a freak, who reveals to us our own "freakishness." That is why many of us are repressive and cruel to the "artist" whom we have banished to some miserable garret of the psyche. We fear and so dishonor the artist within us. We also persuade ourselves that we are ungifted. In some areas, of course, we are, but not in the one area that matters—in being a fellow poet with God of our lives.

How many of us are "normal," normal in the sense that we come from or are now part of a home where mom stays at home, dad works, there are a couple of kids, and they all go to church? Very few of us fit this description of "normal." Is it any wonder we need looking after? Is it any wonder we need tradition, memory, and ritual to keep us on track? How many of us are willing to enter the story consciously rather than have it lived through us unconsciously, and through the distorted vision of a Hitler or a Jim Jones? Who of us has the courage to follow his or her bliss? How many of us have a clue what that bliss might be?

Memory and Perspective

Let us ask ourselves the question, Are we genuinely on pilgrimage or are we simply playing in the sandbox of spirituality? Is our voyage one that only simulates danger? Or are we on the high seas with countless fathoms beneath us?

Studs Terkel tells the story of a television anchorman in Cincinnati who approached him and said, "How about a bite?" Terkel, who knew the city well, was quickly thinking of some delicious food in one of the ethnic neighborhoods. Perhaps some duck with red cabbage? The glazed look in the anchorman's eyes told Studs he was on the wrong track. It then dawned on him that he was being asked to contribute a thirty-second word-burst for an ephemeral television show! Our attention span has now been reduced to thirty seconds. There is no sense of story and tradition, no memory to speak of, and no real grounds for celebration. There's a great deal of dismembering and very little remembering. The sense of the sacred has been lost.

We are now living in instant America, and that goes for art and religion too. We are the nation that invented "fast" everything. We not only have McDonalds, we also have McGod, McPrayer, and McMinister. The result is that we're a little short on memory and perspective—two pillars of the creative imagination and of moral responsibility. Most people don't connect memory and perspective with the creative imagination and the affirmation of the holy in everyday life.

I think that is what blasphemy is—the deliberate ignoring of (or ignorance of) memory and perspective. Images and symbols connect things together. A thirty-second news bite won't do. You need to know the story from which the images have been taken. This takes the time and work of the artist.

In Gabriel García Márquez's fable *One Hundred Years of Solitude*, there is a tribe stricken with a devastating plague of insomnia. The sleeplessness leads to such forgetfulness that the members of the tribe even forget the right names of things. They fight the plague by writing down the names of things that they need to remember on the things themselves. The amnesia becomes so bad, however, that they eventually forget how to read. This decline—sleeplessness to forgetfulness to illiteracy—is what we now suffer in our culture. We not only do not know, we do not know that we do not know.

To be human we need perspective, memory, and ritual. Modern society is short on all three. There has been a quantum leap across the great divide that separated us from recent history. Today people do not even know or care that they are ignorant. The present is all that counts.

We too suffer from a plague that has caused us to suffer a colossal loss of memory. Many of our children do not know who Adolf Hitler was. Ignorance and bigotry go together. The battles of the 1960s are already forgotten. The victories once taken for granted may have to be fought for all over again, but with a blank sheet where there was once a tradition. Of course, the great thing about starting again in California is that you don't need a past! "Amid the encircling balm, nobody is anything for long, let alone for ever."[6] (I read recently of a man rummaging through his parents' attic. He came across an album lavishly emblazoned "This is Our Life." It was empty! A perfect image for our age—a lavishly bound but blank book.)

Ministry Is Re-imagining the World

How far is our cultural and social mess attributable to our lack of creative imagination? Think what it took to imagine India and Pakistan in 1947. Think what it's going to take to re-imagine South Africa, Central America, the Middle East, Northern Ireland, Eastern Europe, and the Soviet Union today. With regard to Europe, some believe and hope a new united states will be born before the end of the millennium. We would be naive and irresponsible if we tried to divorce what we are discussing here from the harsh world of politics. We are concerned with the re-imaging of the world. That is the job description of the minister (ordained and unordained)—to re-imagine the world. The question is, to what end?

The truly creative imagination rescues us from the darkness of a merely private reality. This rescue operation is the sacred function of the imagination in that it puts us in touch with the really real. It is always grounded in awe and worship. There are always rituals that enable and celebrate its work. They also protect us from being destroyed by the fire and passion in our contact with the divine. Remember, when Uzzah touched the ark to steady it, he died! King David cried, "How can the ark of God ever come to me?" How can the human and the divine come together without madness, absorption, or destruction?[7]

We must therefore acknowledge that the life of the imagination requires an honoring of its sacred function. This involves an appreciation of its connection with the collective memory and the means to celebrate those connections. Ministers have to be walking a Path or following a Way. They are called to appreciate the continuum of human experience and to be receptive to it.

Let me give you three examples of what I mean. The first is from a short story by Anton Chekhov that illuminates the power of tradition; the second is a plea for us to balance our market economy with the restoration of a gift economy of which our bread breaking (the eucharist) is a sign; the third is the example of A. A. Milne's *Winnie the Pooh,* which reminds us of the need for playfulness.

The Golden String Links the Beginning and End of Time

Anton Chekhov wrote a parable called *The Student* about the imagination as an instrument by which the continuity of human experience is honored.[8] It is the eve of Good Friday. A young, pious theological student is walking home through the marshlands. It is bitterly cold. He is thinking about the continuity of the biting winds. "Just such a wind had blown in the days of Ryurik and in the time of Ivan the Terrible and Peter [the Great], and . . . there had been just the same desperate poverty and hunger, the same thatched roofs with holes in them, ignorance, misery, the same desolation around, the same darkness, the same feeling of oppression—all these had existed, did exist, would exist, and the lapse of a thousand years would make life no better."

He comes upon two widowed peasant women huddled by a fire and joins them to warm his hands. He says to them, "At just such a fire the Apostle Peter warmed himself . . . so it must have been cold then too." The student reminds the women how little by little Peter had denied

Christ. He is good at retelling the story. In fact he brings so much life to it that one of the older women is moved to tears. The younger woman looks like "someone enduring intense pain." The narrator tells us that in her time she'd been beaten to a state of stupidity by her husband.

The student continues his journey, very pleased at the way he could bring the story to life. He wonders why the woman wept. It was

> not because he could tell the story touchingly . . . but because her whole being was interested in what was passing in Peter's soul. And joy suddenly stirred in his soul, and he even stopped for a minute to take breath. The past, he thought, is linked with the present by an unbroken chain of events flowing out of one another. . . . When he touched one end the other . . . quivered . . . that truth a beauty which had guided human life there in the garden [with the women] and in the yard of the High Priest had continued without interruption to this day and had evidently always been the chief thing in human life and in all earthly life.[9]

We are part of a continuum, a golden string. Touch one end and the other quivers. Touch the string anywhere and the whole thing vibrates. This is the way all times and places are linked. I felt the string quiver not long ago during a lively conversation with one of my daughters and her grandmother. We were caught up in the world of ideas and with the power of language. For me the room was full of ghosts, full of those who had explored the same territory in their own way. I heard echoes of conversations I had had far into the night with students and colleagues, with family members and friends, over the years. The golden string through time quivered and we were united. Touch one end and the other quivers.

Ministers of the Gift Economy

The second example not only insists that we are part of a continuum of intimate connections but also affirms the giftedness of everything. This is a wonderfully humbling truth for the person open to the creative spirit. The poet knows she is walking in a Way. She knows that what she has is a gift, a gift to be given back.

On the cover of Lewis Hyde's *The Gift: Imagination and the Erotic Life of Property* is *Basket of Apples*, painted at the Shaker Community in Hancock, Massachusetts. The Shakers believed that their arts were gifts from the spiritual world. They knew about making the invisible visible. "Persons who strove to become receptive of songs, dances, paintings, and so forth were said to be 'laboring for a gift,' and the works that they created circulated within the community." The Shakers were and are a "priestly" people. They know they are blessed and know how to share the blessing.

Lewis Hyde's maxim is "Where there is no gift there is no art." A gift is not a thing we get by our own efforts. It cannot be bought. Also, "the way we treat a thing can sometimes change its nature."[10] That is why we feel uneasy about the sale of sacred objects, because there is a sense that their sanctity is lost in the marketplace.

We have then the tension in our society between two economies—a market and a gift economy. While we need both, the latter is more important in our time than the former. Alas, it is very fragile. The minister of the creative imagination is the guardian of a gift economy. The cliché "You don't appreciate a thing unless you pay for it" is only a half-truth. Insofar as we equate payment only with money, the saying is a lie. We do have to pay, but there are many ways to do it.

At the center of Christian worship in many traditions is the sacred meal. It is a free gift. There is room for everyone around the table. There is food enough and to spare. We become *substantial* persons by sharing in this common meal.

Lewis Hyde writes about what it means to be a person of *substance*. What makes people "big" in their community? It used to be true that the "substantial" person was the one who gave away the most, the "one through whom the most gifts flowed." In our market-oriented society "getting rather than giving is the mark of a substantial person." It is very hard to maintain a sense of self-worth in a society that tends to honor those whose products are seen as commodities. We judge people's substance by what they have acquired, not by the gifts they display.[11] Isn't this why the ordained often feel inferior and inadequate? Ministers are "useless" because they don't produce anything consumable. Clergy often suffer from "a disquieting sense of triviality, of worthlessness" for this very reason. We return over and over again to the issue of powerlessness. The artist (the truly human person who knows about gifts and blessings) does not measure personal worth in terms of acquisitions. In this sense the artist is a "powerless" rebel in our society. The minister revels in the power he or she enjoys when it is broken and given away, like bread.

The Playfulness of the Tao of Pooh

The third example, the importance of taking life as a gift to be given back, is to be found in Taoism. Following the middle and balanced path of the Tao is a way of affirming the importance of artistic simplicity and priestly receptivity.

Benjamin Hoff in his engaging book *The Tao of Pooh* uses the deceptive simplicity of A. A. Milne's lovable bear to illuminate the wisdom of the Tao. The questions we are tempted to ask the artist are all present in this children's classic. Is creativity action or receptivity? Do we make it happen or does it happen to us? What is the relationship of being to becoming? What does it mean to minister?

> "What's this you're writing?" asked Pooh, climbing onto the writing table.
> "The Tao of Pooh," I replied.
> "The *how* of Pooh?" asked Pooh, smudging one of the words I had just written.
> "The *Tao* of Pooh," I replied, poking his paw away with my pencil.
> "It seems more like the *ow!* of Pooh," said Pooh, rubbing his paw.
> "Well, it's not," I replied huffily.
> "What's it all about?" asked Pooh, leaning forward and smearing another word.
> "It's about how to stay happy and calm under all circumstances!" I yelled.
> "Have you read it?" asked Pooh.[12]

The author claims that in *Winnie the Pooh* we have an example of Taoist wisdom from the West. One of his friends is, to say the least, skeptical. Hoff quotes from A. A. Milne's story to make his point.

> "When you wake up in the morning, Pooh," asked Piglet at last, "what's the first thing you say to yourself?"
> "What's for breakfast?" said Pooh. "What do you say, Piglet?"
> "I say, I wonder what's going to happen exciting *today*?" said Piglet.
> Pooh nodded thoughtfully.
> "It's the same thing," he said.[13]

Hoff's friend argues that this has absolutely nothing to do with Taoism and explains that *Winnie the Pooh* is "about this dumpy little bear that wanders around asking silly questions, making up songs, and going through all kinds of adventures, without ever accumulating any amount of intellectual knowledge or losing his simpleminded sort of happiness. *That's* what it's about." "Same thing!" was Hoff's reply.

I like the image of the minister as a dumpy little bear wandering around asking silly questions. There is something intractably "useless" about the ordained ministry viewed in the world's terms, and Winnie the Pooh is a good image of this necessary "uselessness." Humor is very important if we are not to go destructively mad—mad because of an inflated view of ourselves or mad because we have a low or shifting one.

Don't Talk. Look!

As we have seen, a tension exists between the two views of art. Some art inspires, some art confronts. The artist is always struggling with imprecision and imperfection. There is even something impersonal about the process. Yet art is also deeply personal, and for it to be enfleshed, vulgarity and compromise are sometimes involved. This is true not only of art as a separate activity. It is also a commonplace in everyday experience: the tension between the vision and its incarnation. Sometimes it's tragic. More often than not it's funny. Iris Murdoch, in her novel *The Black Prince,*[14] has one of her characters speak of "the bottomless trickery of consciousness." The remark is made in the middle of a conversation about *Hamlet.* There is a sense in which we have no identity without words and stories. In short, we need art to hold us together. We also need it to be able to see.

Is it possible to give the visible its rightful place in helping to define human mystery? Aristotle called the human being "the language-using animal" (and, God knows, I love language), but would it not be better to call a woman or a man "the image-making animal"? We need a shift in consciousness if the sense of the sacredness of the world is to be restored. We need a movement away from the ear to the eye. We have too many words and not enough of the Word. We are dominated by a corrupt and diseased rationality, by a belief that reason is sovereign and autonomous. We need help to be able to see again.

Feminists are right to point out that part of the pernicious triumph of a wounded patriarchy is to blind us to what there is to see. The best feminist strategy is to get people to see what's right there in front of them and then challenge them to describe it accurately. When we truly begin to see, language will have to change and become more inclusive, because we will begin to celebrate what we see by naming it more accurately.

Humphrey Carpenter writes about a literary promotional tour with Antonia Fraser and their visit with a group of physically handicapped people: "Another woman, in her early forties, has had a stroke so severe that she cannot speak. She writes stories instead. Her husband, collecting her at the end of the afternoon, observes to Antonia: 'Until she lost the power of speech, she didn't have much interest in the arts.' That evening, back in the front of an ordinary audience . . . I have the feeling that it may be we, the able-bodied, who are handicapped in this respect."[15]

Those are stunning words—"Until she lost her power of speech, she didn't have much interest in the arts." The artist is frightening because he or she is an anomaly—handicapped. The minister is "handicapped" too. Anomalies, particularly human ones, stretch our understanding of what it might mean to be human and to be moral. The artist knows what it is to be brought to the end of one's tether, to be reduced to waiting for the gift.

The Minister: Image-Breaker
and Image-Maker

It is often at the moment of utter helplessness that something new begins to explode in us. Sometimes the explosions are violent. Sometimes things get smashed.

The minister, like the artist, is an image-breaker as well as an image-maker. Image making and image breaking seem to be two important human pastimes. I am profoundly moved and disturbed by our longing to smash images. This is what all reformers try to do. Liberation movements want to smash the idols that imprison us. They see the imagination enslaved by images that diminish and destroy. Iconoclasm is very important. The disturbing question is, Do iconoclasts know what they are doing? Why do human beings need to destroy things with such gratuitous violence? Why must certain images be cleansed and put to the flame? Is it because images have too much power, or not enough? Who is controlling the images that control us?

Liberals want to smash the idols of a repressive and irrelevant past. Conservatives want to smash a "gaudy and threatening present." Some ministers come on as great destroyers of illusion and falsehood. Others seek to bring healing images to every human situation. We need both. Ask yourself what you would like to smash. It will lead you right to the depths of your soul. Ask yourself what kind of world you want to create. It will bring you to your knees.

It cannot be overemphasized that the creative imagination always needs grounding in a tradition and rootedness in a community. I need com*pan*ions. I need people with whom I share bread (*panis*). I need nurturing by a community that will share its bread with me as a gift. I am appalled by my fragility and comforted by the fellowship that vulnerability brings. I will go mad if my life is merely monologue. Richard of St. Victor wrote that imagination when distracted "is like a decrepit old man or a senile woman who will drone on without any audience and carry on a conversation as if someone were present."[16]

One test of true creativity is to ask the question, Does it enlarge the world? Does the artist and the work widen the circle of human solidarity? Does it push us toward each other or away from each other? The minister, like the artist, is sure to fail in some measure, because he or she has a double and contradictory task: to reveal the glory of the world and at the same time to show how far we have fallen short of it.

What I would like said of me after I'm dead is, "Above all, he had a sense of passionate solidarity with all people. He made us feel less lonely." Maxim Gorky experienced this feeling with regard to Tolstoy. He saw in Tolstoy's face "something everlasting, near at hand and faraway, divinely earthly and innocently old. Gorky had the feeling that as long as Tolstoy existed he would never feel an orphan in the world."[17] There are one or two people I can think of who assure me by their very presence that I'm not an orphan after all.

A comment by Carl Jung comes to mind: "If I accept the fact that a god is absolute and beyond all human experience, he leaves me cold. I do not affect him, he does not affect me. But if I know, on the other hand, that God is a mighty activity in my soul, at once I must concern myself with him; he can then become even unpleasantly important, and in practical ways too."[18]

Enlarging the Circle

I need a tradition and a community to provide some sort of interpretive container for this "mighty activity in my soul." We need an overarching vision, a regulating and liberating image of ourselves and the world. A. N. Whitehead wrote, "Evil is the brute motive force of fragmentary purpose, disregarding the eternal vision." Without a vision of human community, the art of ministry degenerates into spiritual masturbation— "ipsation" (*ipse* = self), the old manuals of moral theology called it—a self-referential and self-isolating activity. Ministry can often be simply little people enlarging themselves by going around "doing good." True creativity, on the other hand, is bringing to birth something new, something to be shared.

A folktale from Kashmir tells of two Brahmin women who attempted to fulfill their obligation to give alms to the poor by simply giving alms back and forth to each other. They denied the whole spirit of almsgiving. "When they died, they returned to earth as two wells so poisoned that no one could take water from them. No one else can drink from an ego of two."[19]

The truly creative spirit seeks to enlarge the circle of the gift so that all may drink. William Blake, on the day he died (12 August 1827), lay in bed singing songs "so divinely, so beautifully, that [his wife] Catherine got up to listen better, and then he turned to her and said, 'They're not mine you know. They're not mine.'"[20] All is gift.

The Way of Ministry
Is the Way of Unknowing

Many ministers and priests fall into the trap of thinking that they have to know the answer to all religious questions. Ministers who know themselves live with questions and not answers. It can be very lonely being the guardian of questions in a world that wants only quick and easy answers. The creative moment often happens in isolation, as we wrestle with questions. At the very moment when we despair of anything creative ever happening at all, grace pours in.

What do we do when knowing is not enough, when second- and third-hand experience is not enough, when being a voyeur is not enough? In Thomas Klise's *Last Western,* Willie, a renegade student in a modern computerized seminary, calls himself a member of "The Silent Servants of the Used, Abused and Utterly Screwed Up." Willie, among other things, has traumatized the computer by asking it the question, What is the thirst of God? "Sometimes, late at night, the theories and arrangements did not seem enough for those who still had their plain senses.

After a few months even the very brightest students found themselves coming to Willie's room to talk away the night. They came like patients seeking a cure for that disease there is no name for, the sickness, that overtakes those who know that knowing is not enough."[21]

As powerlessness is a recurring theme, so is a special kind of ignorance. To admit that we don't know is already to be on pilgrimage and to face the disease for which there is no name. The character Jack in D. H. Lawrence's *Kangaroo* "was always aware of the big empty spaces of his own consciousness; like his country, a vast empty 'desert' at the center of him."[22] The minister pays attention to this desert within. It is, after all, the territory of ministry. Paying attention to the desert inside us, the place where the mighty activity of the soul is carried out, is called prayer.

The Ministry of Prayer as Listening

What we might want to affirm about prayer we might want to say of the imagination. W. H. Auden, writing about Loren Eiseley, suggests that prayer is the art and habit of listening. Asking for things is the most popular and most trivial form of prayer. More often than not it is wishful thinking, like asking that two and two make five.

> But the serious part of prayer begins when we have just got our begging over with and listen to the Voice of what I would call the Holy Spirit, though if others prefer to say the Voice of Oz or the Dreamer or Conscience, I shan't quarrel, so long as they don't call it the Voice of the Super-Ego, for that "entity" can only tell us what we know already, whereas the Voice I am talking about always says something new and unpredictable—an unexpected demand, obedience to which involves a change of self, however painful.[23]

How many of us know much about prayer in this deeper sense? It's hard to imagine many ministers listening to anyone. We all talk too much and know too much. It's hard to keep up the pretense of being on intimate terms with the Almighty.

Ministers of Grace

The question comes back to that of service. Whom then do we serve? Do we serve a large enough vision that provides saving images that enable us to tell the truth about what has been revealed to us? How much reality can we bear? What is it that enables us to look both horror and glory in the face and not be crippled or destroyed by it? The theological word for it is *grace* or, better for our purposes here, *gift*. The Creed puts it this way: "He descended into Hell" . . . in us and with us so that there are no depths of human experience untouched or unplumbed. In the Christian story, the first act of the Resurrection was to free the souls trapped in the jaws of sin and death. In other words, there is nothing to be afraid of, least of all our powerlessness and our "knowing" ignorance. The imagination is the God-given organ of the soul, able to receive the images of good news about the human condition. Our powerlessness and ignorance are the means by which we know we are related to a boundless mystery.

The imagination, according to Dante, is an image-receiving instrument, not an image-making one. As we saw earlier, it is the faculty by which we look into the reality of things or, better, the faculty by which the reality of things looks into us. That is why the question of obedience and service is raised over and over again: Which image should we choose in ordering our lives? If you are tempted to think that the undisciplined and unregulated imagination is fine, remember Hitler and the mesmerizing way he used images to rally a people in a common cause, in a common horror. His diseased imagination robbed his followers of memory and will.

Practicing the Art of Ministry

A famous collect in the Book of Common Prayer speaks of our needing to "read, mark, and inwardly digest" the Scriptures. Clergy need to learn to do that with people and situations too. The most important skill in the art of ministry is that of being able to read the everyday world of people and events with accuracy. That skill is called discernment. Discernment is the art of arts for ministry. We need ways of telling the difference between the creative imagination and destructive fantasy in people's lives.

An English bishop, late in the last century, told his ordinands to prepare for ministry by reading three things: the Bible, the *Ethics* (by which he meant Aristotle), and modern novels. That is what I try to do. I read the Bible every day, by sharing in the daily office (morning and evening prayer). The mystics of the Middle Ages used the word *ruminare* (to ruminate, to chew the cud, to "inwardly digest") when describing the right approach to the Bible. I admit that I do not read Aristotle's *Ethics,* but I do read books on ethics, philosophy, and theology to keep my mind attuned and alert. I can't read all that I would like to. I have therefore formed the habit of reading on a regular basis the *New York Review of Books, Books and Religion,* the *Times Literary Supplement,* as well as other journals and periodicals. With theological journals, I tend to switch around by changing my subscriptions from time to time. I also read modern novels. Here I am fortunate in having a wife who is much more widely read than I am. She feeds me from time to time with just the right novel. "Alan, it's about time you read this. I think you'll enjoy it."

Reading the Bible, the best of current thought, and modern novels helps me to see the world I share with others. Whenever I get the chance, I go to the theater or visit a museum. The theater holds a mirror up to society, as does an exhibition of modern art. We need to be in touch with the images that form and deform our society. In this way ministers can think, pray, feel, and act with credibility and conviction. Being available to, and yet maintaining a critical distance from, the images we receive from society is part of the work of ministry.

We are constantly bombarded with images, and it is easy to see why the desert tradition of Christian spirituality distrusts images or, rather, pushes us away from sole reliance on them toward silence and emptiness (the desert). There have to be two ways for us to follow: the Way of Images and the Way of the Denial of Images. "We live in silence because the glory of God seizes us and silences us," writes a contemplative nun.

Discernment often involves prayerful hesitation, a kind of wakefulness that is willing to risk. It means being open to one's fears and anxieties. We risk the possibility of both grace-filled moments and destructive and demonic threats when we refuse "to accept timidity in the risk of uncovering the fundamental religious questions in the situation—questions which the very attempt to formulate, however hesitatingly, is always worthwhile."

How do we tell the true from the false, since "truth lies in the interpretation" as the famous double entendre has it? At the heart of discernment, after we have finished "reading" all the texts and people who cross our path, are prayer and adoration. Both are ways of ac-knowledging grace and seeking communion in a caring and corrective community.

Ministers worry too much about filling the churches with people. Nothing would please me more than seeing our churches packed, but God reigns and reaches people whether they come to church or not. We should acknowledge the fact that, in some cases and at certain times, church is the last place a person should go. I am thankful for all the nonchurchy ways God tries to reach me—particularly through music that heals and rejuvenates my soul.

The fact that God reigns in people's hearts and reaches them outside and in spite of "organized religion" drives some religious leaders crazy. Artists, like mystics, undermine authority. They are dangerous. In the end the "word" has to be allowed to erupt from inside us. This is very threatening to the Church, especially its authoritarian wing. But it is also risk-laden for the individual whose "word" may be simply the expression of restrictive fantasy cut off from the truly creative imagination.

The Resurrection of God

I conclude with a statement of my own particular belief. For me the creative imagination is regularly energized by the Spirit of Christ. Christianity provides the architecture of my thoughts. But there are other ways of expressing it. All paths meet not in identical formulations or even experiences (who is to say a Christian's experience of even emptiness is the same as that of a Buddhist?) but in the waiting, in the compassion, in the loving solidarity, in the silence. In the end we all discover that imagination (the ground of which is grateful and radical amazement) has a moral purpose, freedom.

Each tradition has its expressions for the overarching and regulating Image that is Love—unity in unimaginable diversity. The three great images of Christianity, for example, are of the Pregnant Woman, the Broken Man, and the revelation of God as a Community of Persons. All three are celebrated in a sacrament, a sacred meal that honors our preg-nancy, heals our brokenness, and calls us into a community of love.

We don't want something we "only imagined." We want the thing itself. The Tao or Way of which I speak can be discerned in a look, a look described by Charles Williams in *Shadows of Ecstasy*. In one scene the archbishop of Canterbury is celebrating mass.

> It was the look of a man conscious of the gravity of the work before him but conscious also of an entire capacity to deal with it. But was this also the work of cutting and setting right and binding? Was it possible, if less usual, to restore a man's will as to restore his stomach? . . . The Archbishop went to the altar, genuflected and returned, bearing the sacred gifts . . . his voice lingered on and intensified the formula of two thousand years, the formula by which Christendom has defined, commanded and assisted at the resurrection of Man in God.

In spite of the old-fashioned language, this is not a bad definition of the task of the man or woman who carries out the work of ministry: to assist in the resurrection of God in our sisters and brothers.

CHAPTER EIGHT

The Minister as Actor

M inisters practice their art by acting. We are in a form of show business. Public figures are scrutinized to the point of absurdity. One summer I decided to shave off my beard, a fact found worthy of comment in the gossip column of the *San Francisco Chronicle*. This has its funny side, but to be under such a microscope is stressful. People's expectations are often unreasonable, and the Church is ill-equipped to cope when ministers sin and make a mess of things.

Yet I love the confusing world of the ordained, and human beings couldn't live without the ministry of the professional clergy. People need us at the turning points in their lives. At a birth, a marriage, or a death, they look for a blessing. They also look for sacred places. And for these things human beings require institutions, organizations, and hierarchies.

As dean of a lively and challenging cathedral in a city that is wildly secular, I find myself carried along by others who are increasingly aware of their own call to ministry. They know how to bless. They are always looking for ways to give themselves away. Serving as dean of a cathedral is like being the mayor of a small town or being a show-business impresario or being the guardian of a great cave/mountain/ark in the middle of a busy city. Whether they know it or not, people need a cave, a mountain, an ark, in short, a holy space, to be fully alive. They need places where blessing is a possibility. Without such places they die spiritually. It used to be fashionable in some circles (mainly in seminaries) to laugh at clergy who saw themselves as shrine guardians. I know I contradict myself, but that's what we are, guardians of sacred spaces that remind people they are blessed.

Ministers come to grief when they look on what they do merely in professional terms. Ministry cannot be reduced to job descriptions and pension plans (although these have their place). When we lose the sense of the sacred, we have lost everything. I was recently at an ordination service. The church was packed. There was a spirit of excitement and expectancy. A great many women and men were being ordained. I prayed for them. I wished them well. I also worried about them. There just weren't enough positions for all of them. If they expected ordination to be a ticket to a career of ever-upward mobility, financial stability, and social status, they were in for bitterness and disappointment.

Many priests and ministers have been hurt and even ruined by false expectations. A clear vision of the nature of ordination can avert great pain and disillusionment. Christianity turns out to be just what the New Testament promised: crucifixion and resurrection, sacrifice and delight.

Being a Public Figure after an Earthquake

In the mainline denominations we have experienced an upheaval. "In Colonial times, American religion meant the Episcopalians, the Congregationalists, and the Presbyterians. . . . Today, there are more Roman Catholics in America than all three combined, more Muslims than Episcopalians, more people who identify with the Hindu method of transcendental meditation than Presbyterians. American religion now has . . . a new map."[1] Many of us now find ourselves on the margin, when we were once at the center. This has had a profound impact on the way I understand myself and carry out my ministry. The need to make sense of things and to recover my first love may have something to do with age and with our being near the end of the millennium. I was born during the worst period of the Second World War, of English working-class parents who had little education. My children would find the world I grew up in as alien as the planet Mars. My parents were suspicious of religion because they saw it as an instrument of the people who ran things. Clergy were central public figures. They were agents of the establishment, collaborators with the enemy. On the whole, my parents were right. Their world seemed a clearer place than ours now, in spite of the war then raging. You knew exactly where you stood on the social ladder. Things were well ordered, including religion. The road was straight and narrow. The kind of Christianity I knew in England in the 1940s was very different from its manifestations now.

A Renewed Respect for Tradition

In the past thirty years, I have experienced, valued, and rebelled against the insights of Freud and Jung. I now live on the edge of New Age spirituality in a great supermarket of religious beliefs and practices. I am also surprised to find in myself reservoirs of unrepentant conservatism. I value tradition. Is it just my age? I don't think everything going on within me can be blamed on my age. I respond to the sacredness of places and have often seen the impact a cathedral or church can have on the soul. I like churches that are so cared for that I feel moved to kneel down in adoration. There seem to be precious few of them around. Some of my disappointment with the Church has to do with this loss of a sense of sacred space, and with the silence and stillness that goes with it. I am genuinely puzzled by those ministers whose churches look like movie theaters and whose services are devoid of moments of silence. I honestly don't know how they cope. I feel called to bear witness in a public way to what may seem obsolete, to mystery, adoration, silence, transformation.

One summer I got in touch with something deep inside me when my son, daughter, and I lit candles in Notre Dame in Paris for those we love. Such old-fashioned practices serve a need, a need of which we are scarcely aware. I was moved to tears at the Festal Mass of Saint John the Baptist in the cathedral in Florence, which fed me and connected me to something infinitely loving and mysterious.

Almost anything can be a reminder of the transcendent. A friend of mine, working in Nicaragua, met a Presbyterian minister who had given up eating tomatoes. When he was asked why, he said that every time he refused a tomato, he received a reminder of the presence and power of God. It was like a "bleep" going off in the brain to remind him of another dimension, a deeper reality. I suppose "fish on Fridays" was supposed to do that for pre–Vatican II Roman Catholics. It's a pity we don't have a few "bleeps" in common, so that occasionally we could remember together, and in public.

I am finding that many things act as bleeps to jog the memory. My hunger for God has led me all over the world. I have traveled from England of the 1940s to California of the 1990s only to find that I have moved full circle. It has been a long pilgrimage. I am amazed at the changes that have gone on inside me, and I am puzzled and grateful for the illusion (or is it the truth?) of continuity and permanence.

My armory as a priest is made up of strange and disparate things: a love of holy places, a sense of tradition, the various bleeps that wake me up to God and to others. Bible reading (particularly in my own Anglican tradition, in the context of daily morning and evening prayer), confession, spiritual direction, psychotherapy, simple acts of friendship—all help to keep me on track. Woody Allen once said that 80 percent of life is showing up. That's what I do. I show up, even and especially when I don't want to.

What keeps me going above all are the examples of individual believers and the profound sense of connection I feel with ancient, holy places. Then there are the modern novels that feed me and the writers I know personally, like Monica Furlong and Frederick Buechner. These two have the peculiar gift of convincing me that I am loved all the way through. The mercy of God comes in all sorts of ways, through friends and enemies, through prayer and psychoanalysis.

I am tired of "belief" as verbal orthodoxy. Mine is an anthropological passion, the passion to be as humanly human as possible. I find the Church as an institution very difficult, but I am convinced that we cannot do without it because it guards the secret of being human.

The Clergy Provide a Service

A pastor is called to be in touch with the delight at the heart of things and to communicate it to others. Pastors have to serve publicly. It is hard to do that when people treat one as part of the complex of goods and services of society. As we have seen, there is an unavoidable oddness about the priesthood, and ministers shouldn't expect to be "like everyone else." They stick out at parties. At dinners and receptions they are expected to "give an invocation." They are invited or stumble into people's lives at moments of transition and crisis. Sometimes they are considered interfering, and at others never available. Ministers are expected to marry and bury those who discover that they have a vague connection with the local church or synagogue only at such moments of family need.

Let's face it: the clergy are useful and they are there to be used, not least by those who drag up a tarnished and neglected allegiance to suit the occasion. "I don't go to church anymore, but I was raised a Presbyterian," or "I gave it all up a long time ago, but I was baptized a Catholic"—just enough honesty to make the appeal to the worn-out credentials seem legitimate. To be the manager of a religious convenience store in the spiritual shopping mall of Main Street, U.S.A., isn't very satisfying, unless something deeper is going on.

Before I was ordained I was told that the priest was called to stand out in society, like those monoliths at Stonehenge on Salisbury Plain. Those stones reminded people of another dimension and reality. Priests too were reminders of a disturbing "other" way of life, of an unnerving transcendence that kept invading our comfortable existence. It's a wonderful calling, provided the priest or minister has really taken in what the New Testament teaches about being a follower of Christ. It's not about job descriptions, contracts, and pension plans. It's about losing one's life in order to save it. It's about acting it all out on the real stage of the world.

The Temptation to Leave Out the Nasty Bits

The artist sometimes draws our attention to things that most people do not consider "nice." Religion suffers from being overly "nice." The picture it gives of life is often a distorted one. But life is not all excrement and urine. How do we do justice to the whole truth?

Art sometimes slaps us in the face to wake us up and challenge our wishful thinking. The artist also inspires us with the sacredness and holiness of the world. It is well-nigh impossible to do both at the same time. The minister is committed to the whole truth and yet cannot, obviously, enflesh it all at once or consistently.

In one tradition the guru behaves as disgustingly as possible to shock the pupil into finding his or her own path. Some people are determined to have a sanitized religion. One of my students once told me that he used my first book, *Journey into Christ,* for group discussion, and when they got to my retelling Carl Jung's famous dream of God excreting on the Basel cathedral, half the group refused to go on. There is nothing redeeming in "dirty" talk, but something dangerous happens when religion is made up of only the "nice bits" of life. Then all the dirty stuff goes underground and has a high old time in our psyche. Many men and women are committed to a ministry of "niceness," and wonder why they come to grief.

The minister or priest who struggles to be honest knows something of the tension of these two ways to do justice to the spectrum of human experience. Something given us from the outside, as it were, rises up and meets or collides with what wells up from the inside. One side easily becomes sentimental, while the other often lapses into cynicism. One side says the glass is half empty; the other, that it's half full.

Enlarging the World

Peter Brook's book about the theater, *The Empty Space,* opened me up in new ways. His book is based on the conviction that human beings want contact with what he calls a sacred invisibility.[2] Contact with that sacred invisibility is made through ritual, of which liturgy and the theater are supreme examples. *The Empty Space* is ostensibly a book about actors and acting, but it can be read as a treatise on the ordained ministry and the Church. Brook writes about the role of the creative artist in our common life and our need and hunger for the holy. On almost every page one can substitute the word *church* for *theater,* the *Bible* for *Shakespeare,* and the words *minister* and *pilgrim* for *actor, director,* and *audience.*

The Minister's Public Role:
Bringing Things Old and Things New

Brook's book is a helpful analysis of the delicate relationship between innovation and tradition. It provides a way of exploring the questions (so dominant in the Elizabethan age and now revived in our own), Why have we been given life? Against what can we measure it? To answer these questions we have to be aware of our past and yet open to the future. There is a balancing line that passes through the center of every pastor's heart. Most of us err on one side or the other as deadly and rigid traditionalists or as flaky but equally deadly innovators. Brook understands that tradition can be life bearing and innovation death dealing. What we need is the old continually appropriated in new ways. There is a fine line between deadly illusion and life-giving illusion, between fossilized shape and moving shadow. What is really deadly is to watch anything "in a state of anaesthetized uncritical belief."[3]

In our attempt to tell the truth, there will always be tension between optimism and pessimism. I can remember seeing Samuel Beckett's *Waiting for Godot* for the first time more than twenty-five years ago and being captivated by it and puzzled by the people who found the play pessimistic. Beckett plays with the darkness and impenetrability of human experience in such a way that his plays shed light. Why? Because there is no malice in him. He has a ferocious devotion to the truth. "Beckett does not say 'no' with satisfaction; he forges his merciless 'no' out of a longing for 'yes' and so his despair is the negative from which the contour of its opposite is drawn."[4] The brutal fact is that the longing for optimism at the expense of truth prevents us from finding genuine hope. The minister who wants to tell the truth experiences the tension from within: the tension between the passion for truth and the need to embrace a real and unsentimental hope.

In the Church, as in the theater, we need both "apotheosis" and "derision."[5] We need both the divine manifestations and the farts, burps, and gargles of everyday life. Carl Jung tells of a dream in which the priest in a great cathedral is in a gorgeous procession. His footsteps are dogged by grotesque creatures, and when the priest takes up the chalice in the most solemn moment of the mass, snakes, newts, and other creepy-crawlies wriggle out and slide over the rim. All the crazy, rejected, and unpleasant things in life have to be accounted for and integrated. The tension is broken by laughter.

W. H. Auden once described life as a grand opera played by a tenth-rate touring company. And so it is. We can never account for it all at once. That is why we have to develop the capacity for being able to tolerate competing visions. We are often defeated. We often make fools of ourselves. Our straining to tell the whole truth and to dare to hope has its funny side and comes from a shared need, a need that artists like Samuel Beckett understand intuitively. Beckett's audience all over the world "laughs and cries out—and in the end celebrates with Beckett; this audience leaves his plays, his black plays, nourished and enriched, with a lighter heart, full of strange irrational joy. Poetry, nobility, magic— suddenly these suspect words are back in the theatre once more."[6] Shouldn't these words apply equally to the Church's acting out the drama of the Passion? What better way to describe the desired effect on those who have participated in the worship of God, to be possessed of a lighter heart and to be full of a strange, irrational joy.

Brook writes of the theater as *deadly, holy, rough,* and *immediate.* So it is with the Church, which can be all four things. Its ministers too. The Church can be a place of terrible deadliness or awesome holiness. Our experience can be darkly disturbing and strike like lightning. All that ministers (like actors) have at their disposal is the instrument of their art, their own fragile self. W. H. Auden wrote about the peculiar mystery of human identity. What do we mean when we say, "I am"? And how is the "I" brought into being? When we claim that we are (individually and collectively) made in the image of God, we are saying that each one of us is a unique being who can say "I." But more than this, we are also saying that there can be no "I" without "we," no "me" without "us." One way to put it is to assert that each one of us is an incarnation of all humankind. As "persons we are called into being, not by any biological process but by other persons, God, our parents, our friends and enemies."[7]

We are called into being not merely by a biological process but *by other persons.* The actor (and the minister) is able to play various roles, roles that will call us into being as persons. A great evening in the theater is often the occasion when the audience ceases to be merely entertained and is taken out of itself and into a different and larger world. The experience is never "nice." It is *katharsis,* a cleansing by means of a dramatic action. When I see, or, better, participate in the performance of a good play, I leave the theater with a different and deeper interpretation of myself and my life. I can say "I" in a new way. The minister, like the actor, is called to be one of the instruments by which we are transformed.

The Minister as Entertainer
in the Deadly Church

At the beginning of the century Herman Hesse complained that there was far too much entertainment and not enough joy.[8] What Brook writes about the theater might well apply to the Church: "All through the world theatre audiences are dwindling. . . . The theatre has often been called a whore, meaning its art is impure, but today this is true in another sense—whores take the money and then go short on the pleasure. . . . A true theatre of joy is non-existent."[9]

The distinction between entertainment and joy is an important one. Joy suggests risk, delight, and even sacrifice. It requires participation. Entertainment is passive, risk-free. It is designed not to touch the abyss within. Sometimes entertainment is appropriate, but as a steady diet it leaves us spiritually sluggish and half-dead.

Even in the best of churches with great music, preaching, and liturgy, we occasionally experience the same alienation that we do from the performance of Shakespeare. The Church, like the theater, fails to reach large numbers of people even with the best it has to offer.

Some clergy find themselves imitating a role that they learned from a master of the art but in a style long since dead. That is why it is easy to imitate and make fun of the artificial way clergy often talk. What do people do when they want to imitate a priest? They look stupid and put on a funny voice. Like all caricatures, what is depicted is cruelly unfair, but the daft look and the sepulchral voice do reflect an important problem for the ordained. Instead of finding our own way to minister, we try to reproduce or copy a particular style that is alien to us. We need roles to copy and mentors to follow, but at some point we have to make the role our own. More often than not we find ourselves playing a role in a style that we have not genuinely appropriated for ourselves.

Over the years I have met clergy trapped inside a model for ministry that is neither joyful nor life bearing. They are like ham actors re-creating an old role that once had life but which constant repetition has rendered absurd. We find ourselves trapped in a ministry that is all mannerisms and no substance.

I can remember a very "jolly" clergyman when I was a boy whose stock response to everything—even to bad news—was "Excellent! Well done! Jolly good!" We would put him to the test by telling him of a fictional aunt who was dying of cancer. "Well done! Jolly good!" was his reply. He was playing the role of a clergyman, in this case the part of a daffy priest in a British farce. The role didn't fit very well, and the only way he could play it was by being inattentive and only half-present to what was really going on.

The bizarre spectacle of child evangelists mimicking the stock phrases of their vindictive elders in consigning their fellow students to hell is an example of deadly religion at its worst.

The Minister's Field of Work

The actor has himself as his field of work. So it is with the minister. Everything that happens to the minister, all the inner as well as the outer events, is the raw material of his or her craft. Ministry, like acting, is a life's work. In the life open to God there are no secrets. Just as the actor does not hesitate to show himself exactly as he is, so the minister is called to be unafraid of being laid bare.

The actor "realizes that the secret of the role demands his opening himself up, disclosing his own secrets." Acting is a form of sacrifice, of sacrificing what most people prefer to hide. This sacrifice is the actor's gift to the spectator. "Here there is a similar relation between actor and audience to the one between priest and worshipper." The actor invokes, lays bare what lies in everyone—and what daily life covers up.[10]

The strange thing is that we bump into our need for and reliance on tradition at those very moments when we think we have sacrificed everything or have been working with our own resources. The actor discovers that when she tries to communicate "the invisible meanings" of the text of a play, she needs both concentration and willpower. She needs all her emotional reserves. She needs courage. She needs to think. Above all she needs form. It is not enough to feel passionately. There has to be a container and a reflector for her passion. That is why we need texts, customs, and institutions—public things. The person who is both ignorant and disdainful of form is like a child with a box of paints. The child is free to mix all the colors together, and the result is a muddy brown-gray mess.[11] The minister is liberated by forms, customs, and traditions to be a prism through which many colors play. The clearer he or she is, the more the saving power of the sacred shines through.

Ministry as Rebellion: Laughing at the "Holy"

If we are committed to tell and live the truth, we should not be surprised by acts of apparent "irresponsibility." If the new is to erupt

with freshness and life, we allow for the possibility of rebellion and opposition, of anger and even hate. There also has to be an appreciation,
without fear, of the absurd. The Church, like the theater, is a silly place,
"grotesquely clumsy," often inadequate and sometimes pitiful. These are
hard words for the conventionally religious to hear, but the need to make
fun of or get angry with our pretensions and posturing is nowhere more
vital than in the area of religion. Its equivalent in Brook's terminology is
"rough theater," with its promise and threat of unpredictable violence.
"The wish to change society, to get it to confront its eternal hypocrisies,
is a great powerhouse. Figaro or Falstaff or Tartuffe lampoon and debunk,
through laughter, and the author's purpose is to bring about social
change."[12] "If the holy makes a world in which a prayer is more real than
a belch, in the rough theatre it is the other way round. The belching,
then, is real and prayer would be considered comic." Because the rough
theater "admits wickedness and laughter, the rough and ready seems
better than the hollowly holy."[13]

Shakespeare's *Measure for Measure* is a good example of the bringing
together of the holy and the rough in one dramatic work. It also has
much to tell us about ministry, since one of the leading characters claims
a holiness that he doesn't have. The play is set in the base, corrupt, and
stinking world of medieval Vienna. There has to be a feeling of roughness
and dirt for the play to work. Although much of the play is religious in
thought, the thinking has to be done in the context of the bawdy humor
of the brothel. The play features both fanatical chastity and the flesh-
and-blood goings-on of Vienna's underworld. The rough stuff is written
in prose, the "holy" scenes are in verse. Brook writes, "If we follow the
movement in *Measure for Measure* between the Rough and the Holy we
will discover a play about justice, mercy, honesty, forgiveness, virtue,
virginity, sex and death: kaleidoscopically one section of the play mirrors the other; it is in accepting the prism as a whole that its meanings
emerge."[14]

The Church too is a prism through which the whole of life shines,
the seedy and the sublime. We need to be as much in touch with the
rough side of life as we are in touch with the holy. The two are not as far
apart as they seem. Where else should they meet first and firmly but in
the heart of a minister, in the heart of one who has begun to accept the
wonderful grace of God in a cycle of song and suffering? The rough and
the holy meet in the heart of a minister.

Dressing Up and Playing a Role

We need ordinary events to become "occasions." That is why we dress up for birthdays, weddings, and funerals. We feel hurt when someone fails to have a sense of occasion. My showing up to perform a wedding in Grace Cathedral wearing sneakers and jeans would sour the occasion for the bride and groom. In another setting that kind of dress would be appropriate. A great deal of life is dressing up and playing a role. Our lives require choreographing and costuming.

This is not inherently phony. In fact, it is inherently necessary. Spontaneity has to be prepared for and planned. Joy, laughter, and delight take practice and hard work so that when the truly spontaneous happens, we know how to respond gratefully. The apparent effortlessness of a great pianist's performance is undergirded by years of dedication and hard work. True spiritual discipline, far from setting us into a rigid pattern, continually prepares us for the coming of the new.

The Church, like the theater, needs to be in a state of perpetual reformation. We need to make room for sacrifice and delight. How much will it take to convince us that human beings need the sacred and the holy? The Church, like the theater, has to fight for its life in society. I am not talking about the big orchestrated Broadway "hits" that make millions. I refer to the real acting companies across the country trying to make ends meet. They cannot assume that the audience will show up and hang on every word. Brook insists that the actors have to woo the audience: "It is up to us to capture its attention and compel its belief. To do so we must prove that there will be no trickery, nothing hidden. We must open our empty hands and show that there is really nothing up our sleeves. Only then can we begin."[15]

This advice could well be taken by the clergy. All we have are our empty hands. I was much comforted by his pointing to a strange paradox in his profession, namely, "There is only one person as effective as a good director, and that is a rotten one." A director (a minister too) is sometimes so bad that his incompetence becomes a positive virtue. At first it drives the actors to despair and distraction, but as opening night approaches, despair gives way to terror, which in turn becomes a vital force. It can happen that at the very last moment the actors find the energy and the sheer magic to pull it off.[16] One cannot rely on the director's or the minister's incompetence, but sometimes it works!

CHAPTER NINE

Sacrifice

Sacrifice (as self-offering) is the means and the principle of creation. Ministry is our response to God's loving and sacrificial action. The divine mission is to bring us home to ourselves, to each other, and to God. Our ministry is our "yes" to the divine initiative. There is sacrifice and delight on both sides of the relationship.

The trouble is that the word *sacrifice* carries freight, much of it negative. Sacrifice suggests self-destructive activities that are life denying rather than life affirming. One way to get at the positive meaning of the word is to think of the world as a sacrament. It is a "word" to us, spoken by a creator, and therefore the world has something to tell us about ourselves. Raimundo Panikkar writes, "It is the mystery of the Word which makes Man aware that he is primarily a spoken rather than a speaking reality, a spoken rather than a speaking Word, a receiver rather than a giver, created rather than creator."[1]

This is how the world "works," in a language of giving and receiving, in a rhythm of sacrificial blessing. God calls us by name. Once we have heard the word speak us into being, we too can be bearers of the Word. We can be cocreators with God once we know what it is to be a creature. We can truly bless when we know that we are blessed. The ordained minister is a sacrament, a sign, of what is true for everyone. Our lives too are shaped by this cycle of giving and receiving. Panikkar writes, "The Word is vitally connected with community and communication, and, therefore, those who are not faithful in friendship are excluded from participation in the Word."[2]

The Call to Be a Martyr
for the Sake of the Word

In one way or another all Christian ministers are called to be witnesses to the Word, Jesus Christ. A witness is a *martyr,* and martyrdom is the key to a life that is a cycle of sacrifice and delight. To be a martyr is to be a witness to the Word, which, in the first instance, is best served quietly, over a long period of time. When the time is right, the Word erupts in all its glory and judgment. The creative word is always breaking out of contemplative silence. When we are true to ourselves and to the Word who created us, then "martyrdom" comes naturally.

The physical martyrdom of bishops is not unknown in our own day. The people of El Salvador know of it firsthand. I am reminded of Graham Greene's reaction in the late 1930s to a headline in the Roman Catholic newspaper the *Universe*—"Five Bishops Killed in Spain": "One feels wrong about the Catholic press trumpeting its martyrdoms. You don't *complain* about death of that kind. It should be taken for granted."[3]

I wonder what form modern martyrdom will take? Old patterns are falling away. Older ones are being recovered in a new way. This disintegration is a kind of martyrdom, a kind of sacrifice. There is joy and delight at those moments and in those places where the Spirit is forming us all—the Simons and the Matthews, the zealots and the collaborators —into one people.

False Sacrifice: Martyrdom by Triviality

Some find it hard to be ministers during a period of upheaval and disintegration. Many denominations are sapped of energy by civil war. The partisanship in the Church, its internecine squabbles, drain away its life in a kind of terrible parody of sacrifice.

In the 1920s, Father Herbert Kelly found ludicrous the tests some devised for finding out whether a person was a "true" Catholic. For example, many of his contemporaries thought of "the reservation of the Blessed Sacrament" as the test of tests for the truly Catholic, just as certain kinds of Protestants judge others inadequate if they don't subscribe to a particular theory of the Atonement. When I was growing up, the "correct" theory of the Atonement was that of Penal Substitution (basically the spectacle of an obedient Son, willingly taking our place, appeasing the outrage of an angry Father). I have been with ministers who are still fighting the battles of the sixteenth century. No wonder people walk away from the Church, while her leaders fight old battles.

From the outside both Protestant and Catholic wrangling must seem strange to those who have never heard the secret of sacrifice and delight, the message of death and resurrection. Issues change over the centuries but the mentality is still with us, the advocating of a one-issue orthodoxy.

Being Priestly

As an ordained minister, what should I do? How should I live? As I grow older, the pattern doesn't so much become clearer as deeper. Particular images and pictures predominate. One of them is the metaphor of priesthood itself. By this I refer not only to those who are Roman Catholics but also to the ordained of all denominations. I realize that some traditions have difficulty with the word *priest;* I simply suggest that we all lose a great deal when the metaphor is rejected because of the squabbles about the Christian ministry that arose during the Reformation. As in all things, the various denominations need to listen to one another to learn about Christian ministry. In fact, the word *priest* has a great deal to tell us about simply being human. Priesthood as a metaphor has some application to everyone because it is a prism through which we can look at everyone's calling to be fully alive.

The classic definition of a priest is "one who offers sacrifice." Sacrifice is the act by which something is "made holy" (*sacrum facere*). Priesthood has something to do with our being able to recognize the world as a sacred or holy place and to treat it accordingly. That is why the priest "blesses" people and things. It is a way of reminding us of their sacred quality, of who and what they really are. Blessing is a way of calling a person by his or her proper "name" as an image of God. Priests knows that they are blessed and bless in return. Priesthood, therefore, has something to do with sacrifice and with receiving life as a gift and then giving it back. Priesthood is the art of living gratefully and gracefully in a cycle of sacrifice and delight. I believe each human being is endowed with a priestly character.

The metaphor of the ministry as sacrifice and delight has something to do with what Joseph Campbell has called "following your bliss." Bliss is what we want for ourselves and our children, and the words *bliss* and *bless* are closely related.

Sacrifice at the Heart of Things

Everyone sacrifices to someone or something. If the sacrifice is real and not neurotic, life and joy spring from it. What a human being does is simply to bless. To be human is to be in a great cycle of love—knowing one is loved and loving in return. A fragment of one of Raymond Carver's last poems makes the point beautifully:

> And did you get what
> you wanted from this life, even so?
> I did.
> And what did you want?
> To call myself beloved, to feel myself
> beloved on the earth.[4]

The meaning of the ordained ministry has something to do with binding and loosing, holding and letting go. Love knows when to hold on and when to set free. The gospel proclaims to all, "You are loved and are therefore liberated to love in return." We can love because we are loved. We all enjoy an inalienable dignity that frees us to bless. The circle is complete. We not only enjoy God but we are enjoyed by God in a cycle of blessing.

The sad thing is that many of us who are ordained forget the very basis of our profession. We get cut off and lost. We lose sight of the fact that the primary instrument of ministry is our own fragile selves. I have walked with many of my fellow clergy as they have walked with me, through burnout, disillusionment, moral confusion, and disappointment to deep places of faith and fulfillment.

The emphasis on humanity's basic ministerial character will raise the question, How then are we to live together? We won't be able to avoid questions of politics and social arrangements. We clergy all come back, in the end, to accepting ourselves as we are, frail, human, instruments of something beyond us. That simple acceptance of our creaturely status is a sacrifice for some of us. In short, the clergy have to accept that they are human and that their ministry is grounded in a "priestly character" that was theirs from the beginning. We are all priests of creation, born to praise and give thanks, born to bless.

Learning the Simplicity of
Ministry from the Child

Parents know something of the sacrifice at the heart of things. Children need parents who will withdraw and make room for them, to allow them to be. When parents do that, they share in the divine work in the world. God is the One who makes room and allows to be. Parents who fail to do this do great harm. As playwright Lillian Hellman writes: "God help all children as they move into a time of life they do not understand, and must struggle through with precepts they have picked from the garbage cans of older people, clinging with the passion of the lost to odds and ends that will mess them up for all time, or hating the trash so much they will waste their future on hatred."[5]

I sometimes wonder how many ministers pass on garbage or cling "with the passion of the lost to odds and ends that will mess them up for all time." Ministers need help to unlearn the damaging lessons of their own childhoods. Those who do not unlearn them pass the hurt on to the next generation in the name of religion.

It can be fun and illuminating to watch children play with their malleable and forming egos. They play the persona game and are able, unself-consciously, to put on various masks and play many roles. The cartoon characters of Calvin and Hobbes are perfect examples of the game. The little boy Calvin and his companion, his stuffed tiger, Hobbes, go on many wild adventures. The cartoon has wisdom as well as humor. Calvin is learning to relate to the world as a stupendous and wonderful mystery. He knows that he is blessed. He doesn't question it. There is something silly yet sacred about it.

Children's games, however, can become terrifying after a while as children slyly or out of fear put on those masks calculated to deceive, please, or mollify the mother and father. When that happens, something vital is lost. The sense of mystery is covered over, and children begin to lose touch with the energy and joy that drive them.

False Sacrifice to Human
Addictions and Fashions

As we have seen, religion has been corrupted by the shopping-mall mentality and its lazy approach to truth. We go shopping for religion like we would for a pair of shoes. Religion becomes a commodity and loses its power to convey the truth that we are blessed and can bless in return. The ordained are "ordered" into a corrupt and corrupting society, where the notion of sacrifice is already deeply distorted. Sacrifice has come to mean something negative. The emphasis is on the suffering and the giving up of someone or something one wants, rather than on the joy in the release of new life.

What is the remedy? One healing sign is that more and more clergy are aware that they are on a treadmill of sacrifice in the bad sense. The joylessness of their ministry is shown in their addictions (to power, to meaning, and to being right). Many are committed to constant psychological and spiritual cycles of rehabilitation. I often get lost, and the way back to myself is always through the door of self-knowledge by which the human cycle of sacrifice and delight is restored to me.

Another sign of health is that more and more people are willing to be responsible for their own spiritual well-being. Many are discovering their own inner sacredness, and this discovery relieves the ordained of the burden of carrying all the "sacredness" of others for them.

Many clergy fall apart because they sacrifice themselves on the altar of the neuroses of others. They do not know how to cope with people who have become spiritual parasites. This may sound harsh, but one of the problems of religion is that it tends to breed infantile behavior in its adherents. This is not to deny the need for childlike simplicity. In an adult, childlike simplicity presupposes a great deal of maturity and commitment. But the Church often breeds destructive childishness in its members. The spiritual bankruptcy of the mainline (some would say sideline) churches persists, partly because ministers find themselves offering sacrifice to false gods: to the lowest common denominator, to the childishness of the congregation, to the idea that to be a minister is to be a doormat.

When I first arrived at Grace Cathedral, I was a very inexperienced minister in charge of a large church. One day I heard a noise outside my office. A young man, articulate and well dressed, was yelling at two members of our staff because they wouldn't hand out any cash. They had given him a card with the address of one of the church's agencies, but he was angry and frustrated. I led him out of the building to the parking lot. He pointed to my new station wagon and to the cathedral and flung down the reference card at my feet in disgust. "Here you are with your new car and you won't even give me a dollar!" I was apologetic and mumbled something about cathedral policy. Meanwhile another priest was making his way to his car. The young man went straight for him, and I retreated to my car. As I was driving out of the lot, I saw and heard the other priest, his hands on his hips, yelling at the young man, "Don't give me that shit! I worked my ass off for this car!"

I drove home in a daze, trembling with laughter. Yelling that way isn't my style, but I felt that my colleague had probably been more pastoral than I had been. His seemed the more genuinely human encounter. I had been brought up to "sacrifice" my own feelings and allow others to walk all over me, and all in the name of ministry. I'm not advocating yelling and bad language as part of the art of ministry, but the encounter made me think.

Caricaturing Sacrifice

We should never underestimate people's desire to misunderstand the call to sacrifice. Some like to think of the minister as someone representing death rather than life, sacrifice rather than delight. Most people cannot make the connection between the two ideas. The minister is someone to avoid sitting next to on a plane or, if you are a certain type, one to cling to and bore to death with your life story. The various ways people treat the clergy is illuminating: as congenital idiots, paid brainwashers, a third sex, angels or devils incarnate, killjoys, hypocrites, saints. In short, the minister often represents sacrificing all that is human and life bearing.

The trouble is that the pastor represents not only the divine but also the all-too-human. People can be very unforgiving, because ministers tend to fail them on two fronts. They "fail" as signs of loving presence by revealing a God who wants blood. Religion can represent the nasty, mean-spirited side of life. They "fail" when they reveal their frail human-ity. I have met many people (particularly secular humanists) who want me to be remote, slightly dotty, and dependably wrong. Some people want ministers to hold out to them the idea of sacrifice in the wrong sense so that they can then smugly repudiate it.

In a sociological sense we might define the minister as the one who controls, celebrates, and regulates the images that shape our self-understanding. We shouldn't expect people to be grateful to us for hold-ing up a mirror to them.

Who Are Society's Real Ministers?

In that broad sense we might ask, Who are the "priests" of our culture? Politicians, movie stars, rock musicians? Since the priest is by definition one who offers sacrifice, we might also ask, Who are the local gods who demand sacrifice? Every priesthood supports a sacrificial sys-tem. There seems to be nothing wrong with different people taking on the priestly role for society. The question is are we being manipulated or liberated by their "ministry"? Which gods are being served?

These questions aren't merely academic. The nearer we approach the end of the twentieth century, the more (I believe) people will be open to religious and psychological manipulation. People will be sacrificed, psychologically and spiritually, to false gods. People like easy answers to painful human problems, and nothing is more attractive than the prom-ise of an end with the hope of a new beginning. We will need people who have a sense of the sacred if we are to combat the destructive crazi-ness that accompanies the end of a millennium.

As we approach the end of this century, there will be calls for un-usual sacrifice. Our values will be turned upside down and our way of life not only challenged but altered by the pressures of the time. It will be a time for us to recover the sacred vision of human life and bless what there is for being. We all long for the space we inhabit to be sacred, to be "really real" (to use Mircea Eliade's phrase). To be fully alive as human beings demands our living in sacred space. The ordained ministry is a way of keeping the question of the sacred alive, the question of what it means to be a human being.

134

The Clergy's Resistance to Sacrifice

It would be naive, however, not to acknowledge the clergy's resistance to both their calling and to their own inner nature. As we have seen, one thing we resist is the fact that we live in the presence of a limitless mystery. We clergy are the servants of a boundless horizon. Karl Rahner writes persuasively about our resistance to "this unnamed and unsignposted expanse of our consciousness" in which there "dwells that which we call God."[6] We are free to let the matter drop, of course. We can try "to ignore the night that alone makes our tiny lights visible and enables them to shine forth." When we do that, however, we act against our own ultimate being. We become disoriented. We turn away from the boundless mystery to which we are related and to which we owe our being. This boundless mystery is not "some extraneous luxury but the condition for the very possibility of our everyday knowing and wanting." The "sacred person" in each one of us knows and loves this.[7]

Believing and Disbelieving

A. N. Wilson's *The Healing Art* is about what happens when we are thrown into this boundless mystery, the realm of sacrifice and delight.[8] Two women receive the news that they have terminal cancer. The difference in the ways the two women take the terrible news is striking in that it expresses two ways of looking at the world. For them, "the nightmare had happened. . . . The dreadful words had been spoken. The surgeon's knife had cut into her breasts. The shock brought with it a sense of self-loathing and emptiness which was more akin to shame than to fear; it was more like having suffered rape than being under sentence; not de-sexed, but mutilated. Dignity abandoned, they separately fell back on irrational faiths, awaiting what comfort these could yield."[9]

What were these "irrational faiths"? "Dorothy was a believer in modern medicine. Pamela was less sure. She trusted in luck, and the Blessed Virgin Mary and the power of prayer."

You will note that the author describes these as two irrational beliefs. For my part I will always opt for the latter over the former. "Luck, the Blessed Virgin Mary and the power of prayer" sound closer to the cycle of sacrifice and delight than the superstition of "rationality," which is really fatalism. I have seen, firsthand, the power of what we call "luck,"

135

"the Mother of God," and "prayer." These are code words for Rahner's "boundless mystery" and are the instruments of blessing. But then, these things don't make much sense unless you are forced to know (with an honesty that you didn't know you had) that you exist on the boundary, that you are going to die, that sacrifice is demanded of you.

What makes Wilson a fine novelist is his sense of the silliness and profundity of the human condition. He understands how people can believe and disbelieve at the same time. I wish more clergy were aware of this. But then, we are not supposed to admit that there may be holes in the web of our believing.

I think of an elderly priest who was kind to me years ago and who had a great influence on me. He was a fine preacher, but one who needed theological enemies. He loved to make fun of them and to parade his own certainty. He was often cruel and dismissive of others. He wrapped his "orthodoxy" around him like a suit of armor. I never heard him once admit a doubt. He never let ambiguity penetrate his spiritual citadel. There were some truths he could not face. He died in a state of torpid noncommunication in a rest home. In many ways he was a great priest, but he taught me as much negatively about ministry as he did positively. It is hard to imagine this old friend of mine having any sympathy for Pamela, A. N. Wilson's heroine, who "was quite happy to speak *as if* God existed. But she did not, fundamentally, deep down, imagine that He ever actually *did* anything. This troubled her."[10] As for many people, Pamela's was an unthought religion, not deeply believed. Yet the longing was there, as were the glimpses of sacrifice and delight. At least her half-conscious faith helped her live with herself.

Many people exist in the twilight of believing. What surprises me is not that people find it hard to believe but that people will believe anything, and on the flimsiest of evidence.

The Sacredness and Silliness of Ministry

The tension between the pull of the sacred and the sense of the ridiculous is played out in Wilson's characters. Pamela enjoys the friendship of a priest whom she calls Sourpuss. Sourpuss is narrow-minded and opinionated, but for all his faults he knows the mystery of sacrifice. I have met clergy like Sourpuss throughout my ministry. Some seemed hard and bigoted and spoke in an affected way, but they "proclaimed the mysteries with such radiance and which concealed an ocean of kindness so effectively that almost no one would have guessed it was there."[11]

We need people to proclaim radiantly the mystery of sacrifice to us. It is important to grasp the essential absurdity of human beings playing cosmic roles on behalf of others. Even as we grasp the ridiculousness of it, we can also appreciate that we need such people and that they deserve our understanding and compassion. After all, it might be our turn next. Each of us is called to help maintain the world as a sacred place. This is everyone's sacrificial ministry.

The clergy I remember best were people concerned with the maintenance of appearances. I used to think they were hypocritical, but I have come to believe that they are on the right track. People "don't realize that in religion as in everything else, if you look after appearances, the rest will look after itself," says Wilson's priest.[12] For him this was a fundamental principle of life, which had to do with the fact that we are largely responsible for the reality in which we live. If we treat the world as sacred, it will be so for us and, increasingly, for others. If we exploit the world and treat others as garbage, we will create for ourselves a living hell. "What goes around comes around." Sacrifice makes the world go round.

We make our world all the time. That is why the Christian tradition insists on the priority of the will as the center of human identity, and as the altar of our sacrifice. This is alien to us who think that feelings are what really matter. Feelings do matter, and there is hell to pay when we are not "in touch" with them; but the life of the will comes first because we want and need "something much bigger, something easier yet more solid than feeling."[13]

The priest and Pamela have a wonderful conversation on the subject of prayer that emphasizes the need not to sentimentalize religion but to tell the truth. She was concerned that she had to be in the mood, in the right frame of mind for prayer. The priest tells her not to be ridiculous: "If God had to wait for us to get into the right frame of mind, He would be unable to do anything. He takes what little scraps of faith we have and does His best with them."[14]

Pamela found that she liked his way of seeing things, "the way he spoke of the Almighty in the same fashion as he viewed the hierarchy of the Labour Party. Not altogether what one would have chosen, but the best one could hope for in the circumstances."[15] This will sound silly (even blasphemous) to those who want to make their religion out of a patchwork of their better thoughts and feelings. We muddle along most of the time, surprised by mercy and grace. As a minister, I find that I am never closer to mercy and grace as when I break bread at the eucharist, the sanctification of the ordinary.

The Sacrificial Meal: Making Eucharist

I think of the clergy, in all their particularity, who have celebrated the eucharist under all the different circumstances. In the eucharist, sacrifice becomes an act of sheer delight. Elizabeth Cogburn writes affectionately of her father always celebrating Mass "as if it were the first morning of the world." She also writes, "Although I am no longer a member of the church as I cannot abide a she-less God, I do carry a deep love of the Mass, and do proclaim the glory of the Universal Christ in all my teaching."[16] Many wounds need to be healed, and many people feel cut off from the Church. Perhaps the way back is through the eucharist, the sacrament of new creation in which we are all concelebrants.

Dom Gregory Dix, in a purple passage from his *Shape of the Liturgy,* describes the variety of ways the mystery is celebrated. It is worth quoting in full because it is a hymn praising the sacrifice that blesses and re-creates.

> Was ever another command so obeyed? For century after century, spreading slowly through every continent and country, among every race on earth, this action has been done, in every conceivable human circumstance, for every conceivable human need from infancy and before it to extreme old age and after it, from the pinnacles of earthly greatness to the refuge of fugitives in the caves and dens of the earth. Men have found no better thing than this to do for kings at their crowning and for criminals going to the scaffold; for armies in triumph or for a bride and bridegroom in a little country church; for the proclamation of a dogma or for a good crop of wheat; for the wisdom of the Parliament of a mighty nation or for a sick old woman afraid to die; for a schoolboy sitting an examination or for Columbus setting out to discover America; for the famine of whole provinces or for the soul of a dead lover; in thankfulness because my father did not die of pneumonia; for the village headman much tempted to return to fetich because the yams had failed; because the Turk was at the gates of Vienna; for the repentance of Margaret; for the settlement of a strike; for a son for a

barren woman; for Captain so-and-so, wounded and prisoner of war; while the lions roared in the nearby amphitheatre; on the beach at Dunkirk; while the hiss of scythes in the thick June grass came faintly through the windows of the church; tremulously, by an old monk on the fiftieth anniversary of his vows; furtively, by an exiled bishop who had hewn timber all day in a prison camp near Murmansk; gorgeously, for the canonization of Joan of Arc—one could fill many pages with reasons why men have done this, and not tell a hundredth part of them. And best of all, week by week and month by month, on a hundred thousand successive Sundays, faithfully, unfailingly, across the parishes of christendom, the pastors have done this just to make the *plebs sancta Dei*—the holy common people of God.[17]

It is blessing that binds up the world's wounds and makes us into one people. We have lost the vision that the eucharist represents. Ideology, utopian escapism, and psychological reductionism have taken the place of faith in the loving sacrifice at the heart of things. We have lost sight of the fact that the Christian vision transcends the insights of economics, politics, and psychology. This crisis of vision has occurred because our horizon is pathetically limited. In short, we don't know how to bless, because we do not discern the rhythm of death and resurrection in our blood. When we recover the vision of the world as sacred, we will know how to bless. We will know what to celebrate, because we will see the miracle under our noses.

Sacrificial Reality Is Superior to All Fiction

Some people spend their energy inflating their life to the magnitude of the cosmic and mythological. They make their life into a great drama that is boring to everyone except themselves. They think they have to invent themselves. The way of sacrifice is to see the great drama through the ordinary things of life that come to us as gifts and trials. Reality is terrifyingly superior to our fabrications.

In one sense, we don't have to *do* anything, because the symbolic (the Story) is always in the process of becoming flesh, in a cycle of sacrifice and delight. It is not possible to avoid incarnation for long. The Word is always becoming flesh, and human beings are its midwives. The clergy are the midwives of the midwives. We give birth to that which is above and beyond us.

My friend Sister Rachel Hosmer of the Order of Saint Helena died just before Christmas a few years ago. Characteristically her death came as a mysterious gift. Her death invited me to think about what really matters about my life and therefore about my ministry. We first met in 1971 and soon became close friends, later coauthors and colleagues at General Theological Seminary in New York. We didn't always get along. I found her bossy and argumentative, always with a bee in her bonnet. She found me confusing, stubborn, and elusive. She was a fine scholar, a widely sought spiritual director, and a devoted priest.

A mutual friend, Godfrey Wilson (the assistant bishop of Auckland, New Zealand), wrote a poem for Sister Rachel the October before she died. It was a prelude to her death. Godfrey captures beautifully the Rachel our family loved. He also captures the priest in her.

Dying and Healing

You'd sat there by your bed,
talked slowly of a story ending;
the strange grammar of conclusion,
the last letters of life's alphabet.
You'd turned some corners down:
the saving discipline of vows,
prayer's architecture, and the love
of fellow travellers on the way;
dark intervals, when you wrestled
with a self-effacing God
who would not let you go;
the mystery and the laughter.
We'd tried hard not to read
these last lines: the prominence
of bones, the dark veins
under your slackening skin;
tired eyes hinting death,
registering the slow, consuming
march of rogue cells
through your diminished body.
But then you took your pen
and wrote across our wordless
grieving and your pain
this signature of grace:
"It's strange," you said, "how I'm
dying and yet healing,
at the same time.

A death looked at in this way is a revelation. It shows us the life beyond our deadly occupations. It calls us to be participants rather than voyeurs. It calls us to discover our priestly self. The dying person gives us a special moment to reflect on who we are and where we are going, and to pray to the God in whom we believe or half-believe or even reject. On every deathbed is also the gift of hope, the hope of our meeting again, because, as C. S. Lewis wrote, "There are no ordinary people. You have never talked to a mere mortal. It is immortals whom we joke with, work with, marry, snub, and exploit."

We are initiated into the great cycle of blessing begun at the creation of the world. Everything is gift and to live fully is to complete the circle by giving back. In his last book, C. S. Lewis wrote: "And once again, after who knows what aeons of silence and the dark, the birds will sing and the waters flow, and the lights and shadows move across the hills, and the faces of our friends laugh upon us with amazed recognition."[18] What a blessing to be alive. What a blessing to be oriented to a boundless mystery. What a blessing to be human. What a joy to know the secret of sacrifice.

CHAPTER TEN

Delight

God's delight is that we should simply be. It is often claimed that human beings are driven by the desire for power or even by a simple hedonistic urge. I don't believe this is so. What drives us is the desire to *be*. What drives us mad is the desire to be everything. God's delight is to share the divine life with us, so much so that we human beings are called to be the Shepherd of Being.[1]

We were born to care for and nurture being. This may seem somewhat obscure. It isn't if we remember our basic image of romance. Our calling is to delight in the world and to take care of it. This is what we are for. Delight allows things to be. That, after all, is exactly what God did with us—called us into being out of sheer delight.

Making the Invisible Visible

Delight is both the origin and consequence of the sacrificial act of creation, and it is inextricably bound up with our need for and our call to be holy. The holiness of God suggests the awesome separateness and justice of the divine. It's a way of pointing to the "godness" of God. In this context, however, holiness is a way of talking about our need for God and our desire truly to be. To be holy is to celebrate our true identity as God's children and therefore brothers and sisters to everyone. It is awesome. To be the object of God's delight involves the acceptance of the divine justice. That is why we are ambivalent about the call to *be*. We would rather be only half awake rather than fully alive to God's delight. How awesome to be taken that seriously.

How is this basic delight (holiness) made visible? I like the example of the theater, because the stage is a place where the invisible can appear under the forms of all that the visible has to offer—joy and light, darkness and suffering. The theater is the realm of sacrifice and delight. Nothing of human experience need be left out. The liturgy of the Church is also concerned with the miracle of revelation, and the clergy are the peculiar instruments of this wonderful and disturbing visibility.

Think how the delight of music comes to us. It is produced by men and women in evening dress blowing, thumping, and scraping away on instruments made of wood and metal, of catgut and horsehair. In spite of the bizarre way music is produced, we experience, through the art of ordinary people using their clumsy instruments, a moment of delight, a moment of transformation and transcendence. Isn't that what happens in ministry?

Is the Church a place where we can expect an encounter with delight? Do the clergy know that they are its fragile instruments? True, we have many false "delights," one of the most pernicious of which is the cult of personality, a terrible form of idolatry. Many ministers have come to believe that they are the bearers of the transcendent power and delight, rather than its often absurd and always fragile instrument. Delight is recovered not by trying to obliterate the holy and the sacred but by debunking their surrogates.

The Enemy of Delight:
Different Traditions of Ministry at War

Ministers from the various traditions have a long way to go to understand and care for one another. Many of my images for the way I understand the ordained ministry have come from the Roman Catholic and Orthodox churches. Much of the inspiration has come from the Protestant tradition. I can think of no tradition of ministry that has not contributed to my delight in being a priest. I am attracted to the Catholic tradition because it teaches that the unworthiness of ministers in no way invalidates the sacraments they administer, a doctrine that is deeply and liberatingly true. I find myself more on the Catholic side because I need all the help I can get as a Christian, from the liturgy, the sacraments, music. I am not strong enough to be a Protestant. I don't know how my Protestant minister friends can cope going to church Sunday by Sunday. Some of them have to make up the service every week. It seems very burdensome, because what happens depends on them.

I have to be careful that the love I have for my own tradition isn't translated into contempt for other traditions. I have often been closed-minded about other ways of doing things. I have cut myself off from the delight in other traditions. In many ways I think that I am an Anglican out of a kind of weakness. I love the liturgy from the Book of Common Prayer. I like a set text because it saves me from being the victim of the creativity of other people on a Sunday morning!

I suppose each tradition looks at the others with either envy or disdain. While the Church is divided, every ministry is "defective" in some way because it does not and cannot mirror fully God's delight. Perhaps that's why the churches need each other, to reflect the fullness of delight.

A Priest Forever

I'd like to offer an image of ministry that is, in some ways, old-fashioned yet one that transcends our divisions.

I have an Irish-American friend who delights in literature. From time to time he feeds me books. Not long ago he lent me the paperback novel *The Greatest of These* by Francis MacManus.[2] The book came to me through a peculiar succession of events. (Nothing is accidental.) It had been sent to my friend by the Irish novelist Benedict Keily (who had delivered a beautiful tribute to his late brother at an evensong in Grace Cathedral a few years ago). The book was dedicated to Peter O'Curry, a newspaper editor who gave Ben his first regular job in 1940, the year I was born. I mention all this to reveal a sort of "apostolic succession" of events that led to my reading the book and being touched by it. It is amazing how small incidents can get the mind reeling and the heart moving. The smile on a child's face, the hunched and tired shoulders of a mother at the end of a long day, the look of sour surprise on the face of a person who finds that he is suddenly not twenty-five but sixty-five—

all these are windows through which we can see the sacrifice and delight at the heart of reality. And then there are the books that friends give us.

The Greatest of These is a deceptively simple tale, written in 1943, about a bishop who as a boy had been deeply influenced by a priest in his village. That priest had subsequently been ruined by an act of passionate disobedience, had fallen out of sight, and was thought to be dead. The story tells of the loving process of his being brought back into the circle of delight.

Imagine the scene. We are in pre–Vatican II Ireland in the 1930s. It is New Year's Eve, and the bishop is having a drink with three of his priests. The bishop has just heard disturbing news of an old friend from his past, a priest who had deeply influenced the bishop when he was a boy. The priest, to the bishop's surprise, is still alive, but in sad and reduced circumstances. Years before, he had been "ruined," burned by his passion for the priesthood. The priest was now old and a little crazed, cut off from his friends. The archdeacon and canon are arguing the merits of the case of the priest's undoing. "The Canon was saying that it was the case of a man with power who was anxious to use that power to the very limit with the best intentions, while the Archdeacon was demurring and insisting that the man went beyond his proper power."

The reason for the priest's ruin isn't important. At issue in the novel is the bishop's concern for the priest's restoration. Out of the ooze of his half-forgotten theology comes the phrase from the Letter to the Hebrews: "Thou art a priest forever according to the order of Melchisedek." It becomes a haunting refrain that reminds the reader of the indelible character of the priesthood which binds and liberates at the same time. It binds the priest to a particular identity. It liberates the priest into a life of ever-widening possibilities. It is the seal of God's call and delight.

The bishop spends a great deal of his energy looking for the healing word for his old mentor. "He was waiting to hear one, omnipotent, all explanatory word spoken, one word as simple and as huge as the voice of a bell. Yes! One word! There must be one, simple, ineluctable word to bend the rigid strength of one human will, one man's decision—one man who now troubled him as the bells troubled the mild, midnight air."[3]

The healing word is an obvious one. It is love. But this is no easy utterance of a sloppy sentiment. This word requires wisdom, skill, and attentiveness if it is to be uttered truly. The novel is a compassionate account of the weakness of ministry. It uncovers the failure at its heart, the failure of the Cross. It also reveals its true delight, the joy of the resurrection.

"The Truth Shall Make You Free"

A few years ago I had an opportunity to go through an intense experience that made me reassess my life as a priest. I was on the shortlist for the election of the bishop of Los Angeles. Five of us traveled more than a thousand miles and saw fifteen hundred people or more in eighty-four small groups, all in eight days. We were quizzed from morning till night about what we believed.

Well, what did I believe? I found myself coming out somewhat conservative with regard to doctrine and liberal with regard to pastoral practice. I was also horrified by the process. I had no quarrel with the people handling it. The chairman of the search committee was a priest of unusual spiritual depth and kindness. But I found that I had no stomach for the way the episcopate was envisioned. I had no wish to be the chief executive officer of a large and unruly corporation.

I was thrown back to thinking about the first time I fell in love with the priesthood. What did I believe? Was my delight in ministry draining away? My mind went back to the College of the Resurrection in Yorkshire, England, and the phrase "For their sakes I sanctify myself" came back to my mind. I knew that I had to recover my first love if I were to offer myself for any position of leadership.

I came away from Los Angeles with no sense of blaming that diocese for the strange process it put us all through. Still less did I have any reason to "put down" the vocation of a bishop. I simply knew it wasn't for me. I couldn't *delight* in it for me. I wasn't ready and would probably never be. So I withdrew my name.

My heart needed renovation. And, under the mercy of God, I am now in a place that graciously is helping me recover that first sense of delight (and resistance!) which drew me into ministry. I meet more and more people in San Francisco who are in touch with failure and delight, who bring me nearer to my first love. I discover that ministry is something shared with all people.

The Terrible Burden
of Never Having Done Enough

I fell in love with the priesthood nearly forty years ago, and I have been falling in and out of love with it ever since. The recovery of my passion and enthusiasm has been a long and slow process. It began a few years ago with my writing a book on spiritual direction. It was my third book, and I was at the time in psychoanalysis, which for me was a way of being in touch with and living from a feeling of weakness and an experience of spiritual frailty that turned out to be a wild encounter with grace. The analyst began the session by saying, "Well, you've published three books. How do you feel about it?" I laughed and said, "There's a little voice inside me saying, 'You've published three books, why not six!'"

Later on in the session I told the analyst that I sometimes felt hopeless, and he replied, "From what you've just told me your situation is hopeless!" I was tormented by the thought that no matter what I did, it would never be enough. From that date I began a long journey of recovery from one of the occupational diseases of the ordained ministry, perfectionism, of never having done enough. It's a terrible treadmill, and many clergy are on it. Behind the disease of perfectionism lie two terrors we have already encountered—powerlessness and ignorance. I had and have to do battle with issues of power and with the gracious "unknowing" that comes when we know that our basic orientation is to boundless mystery. I do not want to give the impression that I have somehow arrived. I haven't, but I journey in hope. The delight has returned.

The Priority of Love
and the Recovery of Delight

At the beginning, I always wanted to be wiser and better than others, because I had not yet learned to trust my own wisdom. I wanted priesthood to "pay off" in some indefinable way. It was but another manifestation of the issue of power. I wanted it to count in worldly terms. I wanted it to be a career. I couldn't imagine the word *delight* being associated with ministry. I had no idea that it could bring so much joy.

148

What exactly is this mysterious thing called vocation? I think of it as a wild and passionate—even fierce—love welling up in me. It is so powerful that I hardly know where to put myself. I repress it, deny it, accommodate it. A chance remark, a smile, a phrase from a book, the awesome simplicity of the sacrament, almost anything can strike like lightning and release a wild longing I barely understand. I try to rechannel it, but it won't go away.

I found it welling up in me one summer when, for no apparent reason, I thought of a friend, a priest who shares this longing and is impatient with the Church. I had a fantasy that he had died. I experienced a powerful sense of loss and a deep longing to tell him how much I loved him. At the end of this flight of imagination, I was left with a renewed sense of vocation as a priest. My friend would be amused and surprised to learn that he inspires my ministry. It's his delight in life that inspires me.

I think of others who have influenced me. Norman Hook, the vicar of St. Mary's Church, Wimbledon, in south London, in the 1940s, who later became the dean of Norwich. To a nine-year-old he seemed remote and learned, but I still remember the tone of his sermons. He delighted in the intellect. His sermons had a toughness and a love about them that I can still feel. I know that he still influences the way I preach.

Leslie Wright, his successor, had been chaplain in chief to the R.A.F. He appeared hearty, jolly, and superficial. This was an unfair assessment. He had great kindness and depth. He delighted in caring for others. His sermons weren't very learned—usually potted biographies of Victorian heroes like General Gordon and Florence Nightingale. I can remember one sermon based on Charles Kingsley's *Hypatia*. Some of the congregation weren't very kind to him. This was my first experience of seeing the kind cruelty a congregation could inflict on its minister. There was an active group of evangelicals (our parish being merely low church), and I remember one of them (a retired army officer) who suggested darkly that he wasn't sure the vicar was "saved." I was appalled by the facile way this evangelical group was able to play the role of God and separate the sheep from the goats.

The Delight of Ordination

As storytellers, artists, and actors, ministers assist at the birth of new things in the human heart. They are midwives of souls. The metaphor of birth is an important one, because the coming into the world of new life is both sacrificial and joyful. The delight is costly.

The Latin version of the famous verse "God so loved the world . . . " (John 3:16) is "*Sic Deus dilexit mundum* . . . ," which might be translated, "God so delighted in the world that he gave his only begotten Son." The world is based on God's self-giving delight. This is how God works in the world, and God has made us in such a way that we all need midwives to bring us into new and full being. The divine delight comes to term in us through the agency of other persons and their own peculiar history and perspective, which comes into play with our own to make something new. New delight comes to birth in the soul through the interplay of both the old and the new in human experience and in human relationships.

Tradition and Innovation:
The Drama of Delight

We have to be on the watch for enemies of delight. As we have seen, ministers can be in the service of a deadly tradition that gives birth to nothing but a spiritless dryness. They can also be enslaved to an imagined immediacy of experience that produces only wind. A priest whom I saw as a deadly traditionalist accused me of being enslaved to "the spirit of the age" because I was in favor of the ordination of women. I saw him as enslaved to the spirit of a different age. I believed that he and others like him were trying to sustain a "deadly church." He believed that I and others like me were deliberately or unwittingly killing off a lively tradition. Neither one of us could take delight in the other because our defensive postures deprived us of both vulnerability and humor.

An encounter I had with another priest, by contrast, was delightful. He wanted to make his church facilities "totally open" to the community. When I said that to be "totally open" he could run a medically supervised brothel on the top floor and allow the John Birch Society to meet in the basement, he smiled in recognizing that he was more in touch with the tradition than he realized. There were, after all, limits to his "openness." We need the viewpoints of others not only to give us perspective and balance but also to assist in the birth of the new in our minds and hearts.

One great enemy of delight is our attitude to the Bible. There is a pervasive belief that the King James Version fell from heaven, bound and complete, in 1611, and that somewhere, someone found out and defined exactly how the spiritual life should be lived. Everything is prescribed. There is no place for innovation. In some ways the organization of the Church looks as if it has arranged things precisely to see to it that the Spirit is kept in check, to see that nothing happens, least of all the breaking out of delight. Deadliness has a terrible mystery about it because it is not really dead. It is depressingly alive, the active enemy of delight.

In order for ministers to act as midwives of the soul, they have to be prepared to allow for a little craziness, for a certain kind of madness. One way priests can play the role of midwife of delight is to see themselves as directors of a play. Ministers are called to lead the People of God in a particular direction. As actors, storytellers, and artists, ministers are in a sense always "imposters" and improvisors. We are like guides at night who do not know the territory and yet have no choice—we are called to guide, learning the route as we go.

It takes a certain playfulness and trust to make things up as we go along in the context of a lively tradition. The deadly minister pretends it's daylight all the time and uses old formulas, old methods, old jokes, old effects to lead people into dead certainties instead of into a living path. Being fully alive involves uncertainty. Acting from a center of playful delight takes class. It demands real style.

A Matter of Style

The exercise of the ordained ministry, like acting, has to do with that elusive thing *style*. It is hard to pinpoint, but it is unmistakable. I come to the ordained ministry with all the particularities and peculiarities of my upbringing, personality, and education. Add to these my convictions, experiences, and beliefs, mix them together, and you get something of my style as a midwife of persons. God's love for us is startlingly particular. God's delight in us is deeply personal. The miracle of love is that each person is seen as radically unique.

The trouble is that questions of style are often confused with questions of principle. When we don't like something, or when something makes us uncomfortable, we tend to condemn it as wrong, because we cannot stand God's "irresponsible" delight in making so many different kinds of people. What we cannot stand is the provisional character of all our arrangements, especially our theological ones. God delights in us so much that the Holy Spirit is always "making us pregnant" with the new and unexpected by unfitting us for things as they are.

Striking a balance or finding the right mix between tradition and innovation is a tricky business. At Grace Cathedral in San Francisco, where I share my life with a varied and creative community, I cannot afford to ignore fashion, neither must I be a slave to it. How can a cathedral be wildly hospitable to all people and at the same time be utterly true to its tradition? Much of what we do is written on the wind. History is always being rewritten, and the meaning of things is constantly reformulated. We cannot stand aloof from "fashion" or "style." Yet a church can never be just a fashion house. The fact is that one cannot separate the things that never change (eternal truths of love and justice) from the ever-changing modes of expression (fashion and style).

The Church is called to be wildly hospitable to the world without allowing the world to set the agenda. Priests or ministers have to be persons of both breadth of spirit and clarity of commitment if they are to assist at the birth of persons in the cycle of sacrifice and delight.

There are occasional moments when we see that sacrifice and delight are, at heart, one and the same. I once asked a charismatic and wise priest for his blessing. I knelt before him, and he dug his bony hands into my scalp and prayed: "O God, give Alan the wisdom to tell the difference between what is important and what is merely interesting!" It was a moment of rebirth. There was pain and there was delight. In this gracious moment of truth, it was impossible to distinguish between them.

Many clergy are caught in ways of thinking and behavior that cut them off from new possibilities. They become snobs of the "old" or snobs of the "new." This is why I find the artist such a powerful model for ministry. A great performance is always caught in its own time and place. It acts as "midwife" for its own generation. It soon becomes dated. It won't do for the next generation. It is painful to give up what was once a delight for the sake of something better, which in its turn may have to be given up too. Things that give us delight cannot be possessed. They can only be enjoyed and set free.

Laurence Olivier's film of Shakespeare's *Henry V* dazzled me when I first saw it many years ago. Next to Kenneth Branagh's new version it looks like a cartoon. What happened? Fashions and perceptions change, and we along with them. Yet the shifting form is life bearing of something eternal even as it changes and dies to make room for something new. It is not difficult to see how sacrifice is closely related to delight.

An old priest once said to me, "There is nothing you cannot accomplish as long as you don't have to take the credit for it." If that's the case, it won't matter if what I have done and said looks worn out and ridiculous to future generations. I can let go. I can trust. I can take delight. I can laugh. I can cry.

Tears and laughter are two central expressions of being human. They are the outward manifestations of the inner cycle. We know that human beings do not just happen. We are *made*. We are made by our choices and our experiences. We are formed by the stories we tell, the disciplines we embrace, and the schools we attend. Delight breaks in when we begin to connect with one another and see a pattern of meaning. When people are drawn to the story, are open to the new, and are connected with the drama being played out inside them, the Spirit goes wild and the world is healed by the divine delight.

The threefold task of the pastor is to tell the story, to prepare people for the new and unexpected, and to help people connect their own personal and communal story with the greater drama playing itself out on the stage of human history. In the Church, as in the theater, when things go as they should, we can, as it were, see ourselves in action. We can experience the new through the transcendent experience we call worship. In it sacrifice and delight are one.

God's Delight Unsettles Us

Things that in the end delight us are not always pleasant at first. This is why we miss a great deal of life's delights when we distance ourselves from the things that challenge us and make us uncomfortable. Is this distancing a sign of the appreciation of the holy? Or is there behind it a fear that something would be exposed if the light were too bright? Much of modern theater is deliberately alienating precisely because the author and the actors want the audience to wake up and cross over into the action. They want the audience to risk delight by allowing for the possibility of a pregnant moment.

153

Alienation is a process not usually associated with delight. It cuts across and interrupts our view of reality by holding it up to the light. Alienation makes us look again. It invites us to work on ourselves in such a way that we become responsive to a more complete and generous view of life. It expands our capacity for delight. In the theater, alienation is midwifery. A series of alienating events on stage can suddenly confront us with our frailty and lostness.

A little-understood aspect of worship is that it unsettles us and catches us off guard. Through the action of the liturgy we are led into another world, more loving and more just than the one we have left. But we are not allowed to remain there in a lofty and remote idealism. We are further challenged to explore the ways our society can change and move in the direction of the vision that the liturgy embodies. And what is that vision? In the liturgy we learn that the end of all things is a banquet of delights, a table where there is room and food enough for everyone.

How We Are Deepened as Persons

Worship is an act of midwifery for our deepening as persons. The deeper we are, the more capable we are of bearing sacrifice and experiencing delight. On the one hand, we have only our own experience to go on, what we see, think, and feel. But that is not the end of the matter. A kind of negative gift is at our disposal—our horizonless ignorance. The more clearly we see what is missing, the more accurately we experience our lack of depth. The worshiper lives in a realm of a powerlessness that is also potent and is in touch with an ignorance that is the doorway to great wisdom. The art of worship lies in connecting those strands of experience that remain unlinked when we insist on our own isolation. What could be more miserable than to be left entirely to ourselves?

Many ministers (only too well aware of their lonely shallowness) are led to anger, frustration, and despair because they think that what is demanded is omnicompetence. What sustain us are mercy and grace, God's delight in us. What is demanded of us is the humility of self-knowledge. We are called to recognize the missing links in our relationships, the great interstices that only God can fill.

We are not deep enough on our own, nor should we expect to be. We are, however, connected to depths we can never fathom. We are all ministers of these depths. Everyone has a ministry in this sense. We all play different "midwifery" roles in the drama of being formed into a family, destined to delight in one another.

What have we got to go on? The Bible brings together two great worlds for us to explore and weave connections between: the inner and the outer. Some people choose one world over the other, and each one thinks his particular world is complete. In Shakespeare, for example, the two worlds come together. He was able to bring the pattern of events in the outside world and the inner events of complex men and women (the vast tug of their fears and aspirations) into open conflict. "Drama was exposure, it was confrontation, it was contradiction and it led to analysis, involvement, recognition and, eventually, to an awakening of understanding."[4]

What could be a better description of the possibility of new birth as the drama of the Bible is acted out in the liturgy? This is the basic text of the school and method called Christianity. Its purpose? To wake us up and bring us to birth as children of God. Our purpose? To understand ourselves and others as the objects of God's delight. The School of Love brings together the inner and the outer in the formation of persons in community. It exposes, it confronts, it contradicts, and it leads to analysis, it invites involvement, it provides rich imagery for self-recognition. It wakes us up to our true nature and therefore expands our capacity for enjoyment. And it does all this as we wrestle with what Hamlet calls "the forms and pressures of the age." The minister is at the center of it all—suffering and singing, crying and laughing.

The Pattern of Life of the Minister

What do I do to "stay in shape" for delight, to keep in touch with the wellsprings of joy? A friend of mine gave me a framed quotation by William Butler Yeats which sums up what I want to be. "We can make our minds so like still water that beings gather about us that they may see, it may be, their own images, and so live for a moment with a clearer, perhaps even with a fiercer life because of our quiet." It may seem a strange one, but my primary goal is to learn to be still and stay quiet.

Contemplative attentiveness is the wellspring of delight. The philosopher Pascal had the delights of the intellect and heart in mind when he wrote, "It is natural for the mind to believe and for the will to love." Such inner delight that I have been given comes from my feeding the mind and opening my heart. In this way I am set free for action.

Discipline Is for Delight

My delights are specific. I read voraciously and somewhat indiscriminately. I also exercise regularly and try to be aware of what my body is telling me about myself and the situation I'm in.

I take time off. I try, unsuccessfully, to be lazy. I am working at not being a workaholic, and can laugh at myself. Above all, I try to pray regularly the prayer of quiet and stillness.

In my tradition the clergy are committed to reading the daily office, which consists of large portions of Scripture (especially the Psalms). I am lucky to be part of a community that provides opportunities for community worship at least four times a day. I don't think that I would do very well without a supportive and traditional community. I attend and celebrate the eucharist regularly. I have a confessor and spiritual director, and I have been in various forms of therapy.

My discipline may sound somewhat elitist and narrow. I don't think that is a fair assessment, but I can see how it might look that way. We all have our own unique approach to the life of faith. This is what I do with who I am. I need community and tradition. I need friends and colleagues. If I am to be a midwife of persons, I need all the help I can get to think, to feel, and to act.

I find that everything I do, not least my desire to be quiet and still for the sake of others, is marked by a rhythm of sacrifice and delight. There is sacrifice in letting go. The sacrifice of the ego for the sake of both the spirit and the soul is often accompanied by intense pain. The delight is also deep and strong. To feel a birth of new life in oneself and in others is part of the privilege of ministry.

CHAPTER ELEVEN

Song and Suffering

L ife is a cycle of giving and receiving, sacrifice and delight, singing and suffering. Knowing that there is a cycle can help us
wrestle with the forms and pressures of the age. The strange weapons of
ministry are the powerlessness and the ignorance of those who know
they are related to the sacred, to the holy. Such a relationship helps me
to interpret my suffering and my longing and to see them as part of a
cycle that includes delight and laughter.

But who really wants to foster that basic relationship with the sacred? I have been struck over and over again by the modern resistance to
the holy. I used to believe that it was simply a matter of some people
thinking that religion was silly. I now see it often as an expression of the
fear of powerlessness and ignorance.

My own ministry could be characterized as a struggle about power.
I fear powerlessness, but I also fear my skill (and my lack of skill) in using
the power I have legitimately been given. The more I have clutched at
power, the less joy and delight there has been in my life.

The double fear of powerlessness and of the power or improper use
of legitimate power is often found in intellectual controversies both in the
academy and in the Church. The way to combat the fear is to reduce
everything to manageable psychological terms. When everything is ana-
lyzed in such a way that the holy and the sacred become either unnecessary or forbidden categories—the leftover mumbo jumbo of a rejected
past—then life becomes both predictable and joyless. It was hard for me
to come to terms with the fact that my flight from the kind of suffering
that powerlessness brings was also a flight from joy.

No matter what we do, we shall suffer, with and without meaning. If we are awake, we shall also sing and take delight. Sometimes sacrifice and delight meet in special moments of grace when we are able to give ourselves away.

The Retreat from Mystery into the Analytical

English professors fight among themselves about the meaning and status of texts in much the same way theologians did in an earlier era. As Frederick Crews, an English professor at Berkeley, points out, this analytical approach (known as "social constructionism") has a strong hold on many who teach English at our universities.[1] It also holds in its thrall many thinkers and writers who try to make sense of the past. It therefore has had an impact on the way we think about faith. The analytical approach isn't questioned. It is considered self-evident. The assumption is that no value, idea, and person under consideration has ever been able to resist being reduced to further components. The problem is that this assumption must also apply to the person making the judgment on a particular text, value, person, or idea. The person making the judgment must also be reduced and relativized. We end up in a hall of mirrors of diminishing and boring relativizing. Sacrifice and delight are reduced to matters of crude pleasure or pain.

According to this approach, this book is not really about my experience of the ordained ministry. It's really about my coming to terms with my father's death when I was twelve and its subsequent traumatic effect on my early adolescence. What I am really trying to do in this book is to come to terms with my own insignificance in a largely hostile world by using such words as *sacred, holy,* and *priesthood* as a means of giving some semblance of strength to a rather fragile hold on reality. My ordination is really a way of my trying to find the family I never had, etc., etc. etc. ad nauseam.

It is not that there isn't some truth in these interpretations. But what is outrageous and unsubstantiated is the claim that this was all that was going on. The analytical approach trivializes the suffering and drowns out the music of my life by reducing it to what can be easily explained.

We can turn the reductionist "interpretation" of the book on its head, of course, and wonder what nefarious and hidden Freudian impulse led the critic to this particular reductionist interpretation. What dark secret, we may ask, makes people hate the sacred and the holy? The trouble is that those who use this method magically exempt themselves from the same kind of reductionist scrutiny. In theological circles I have heard monasticism reduced to issues of sex and depression and spiritual disciplines to escapism and masochism. Mozart has been reduced to a cackling idiot who happened to write sublime music. Reducing things to manageable proportions may be useful in some fields of study. In the life of the Spirit, reductionism is a form of murderous lying.

We are all victims of our hungers and longings, the minister as well as everyone else. I cannot (nor would I wish to) ignore the fact that my father died when I was twelve. Nor would I deny that his death had a tremendous impact on me, all the consequences of which have not yet been worked through. That death, like the stone thrown into a pool, spreads an ever-widening if ever-diminishing circle of influence. It has affected all my relationships, especially my most intimate ones, and provided much of the music of my life. But there is more to me than that. There is something irreducibly sacred and holy about each one of us.

The social constructionists are caught up with issues of power (which might account for the joylessness of their writing). They do, however, give sound advice. When we study a text, we should give our critical attention to those who came out on top in the power struggle. The winning party will have an ideology by which it justifies its right to dominate "as something ordained by God or nature or history; and the proper function of criticism is to undo that mystification."[2] Our task is to debunk whoever is in power. This is an important intellectual discipline for the study of the past, because God, nature, or history has often been invoked to justify the policies of the dominant group. Some demystification is in order. The cruel nonsense of the following, for example, needed showing up for what it was.

> The rich man in his castle
> The poor man at his gate.
> God made them high and lowly,
> And ordered their estate.

But debunking is hardly a worthy end in itself. What's left when everything has been reduced and flattened? Professor Crews points out a crucial flaw in the social constructionists' approach, their exclusive claim to a skeptical grasp of historical processes. They are the ones in the know about what was really going on in the past. Their job is to remove the mask. Crews uncovers their own unexamined, humorless ideology. They have a "puritanical concern to maintain a politically correct position— one that will be guiltless of sexism, racism, economic individualism, and other distortions of a presumed state of nature. In practice, this spirit of post-Sixties conformism translates into a perpetually scandalized relation to the past."[3]

In California we expect seventeenth-century Franciscans, in their treatment of the native population, to have behaved like twentieth-century liberals. This puritanical "liberalism" has infected the study of religion and our understanding of ministry. People instinctively turn away from this liberalism's reductionist tendencies toward the more conservative churches. Shallow "liberal" religion has little to offer in helping us understand our pain and our longing, our suffering and our loving. In the liberal churches, there are ideologically and politically correct views, and excommunication is threatened if there is any deviation. In a world in which it is "natural" and God-given to be free to break promises (after all, they are only the fabrications of the dominant group) and to pursue and discover one's own personhood, words like *sacrifice* and *delight* would have no place except in a very distorted form.

Ministry Implies Both
Hierarchy and Transcendence

Crews uses two crucial words—*hierarchy* and *transcendence*—which are anathema to the reductionist approach and which have a great deal to do with sacrifice and delight, with suffering and singing. To believe that the universe is "ordered" (hierarchy) and enjoys a purpose beyond itself (transcendence) is to be willing to sacrifice a narrow and private vision of the world for a generous and open one. While Crews is not using these key words in a religious sense, they do, nevertheless, make room for the possibility of the meaningful use of such words as *sacred* and *holy*. They also prepare us to be open to experiences that these words describe.

By transcendence Crews is suggesting that a writer from the past might in some respects be "exempt from the collective unconsciousness of his age." In other words, he isn't simply a blind automaton mouthing

160

the received opinions of his time. He might have been onto something that resists analytical reduction. I think this is what all great art does. In spite of how we might reduce personal behavior, political views, and social beliefs to one guilt-ridden heap, art is the bearer of the transcendent and hierarchical. Hierarchy has to do with evaluating and ordering our loving and our view of the good in society.

Hierarchy is a forbidden word among some feminists because they take it to mean a male, linear ordering of reality. In that sense hierarchy needs a radical critique. But hierarchy, in the sense I am using the word, is concerned with the way reality is ordered, and it refuses to be reduced to the lowest common denominator. That is why art—even in its most negative forms—is the bearer of the holy and the guardian of the sacred, the enemy of reductionism.

Ministers are ordained as a protest on behalf of the sacred. Weeping is one form of protest. Laughter is another. It is a pity that many clergy have swallowed the psychological reductionist pill. A priest friend said to me on his return from work in Africa: "How refreshing to be with clergy for whom life is immediate—serious and joyful—and who don't spend their time mouthing psycho-babble!"

Song and Suffering

The contradiction in the double hunger for the deeper things and for protection against the pain that often comes in their wake is expressed by the poet Seamus Heaney in one of his essays.[4] Heaney poses the question, How can one write poetry in a time of pain and anguish? The two hungers are expressed in the words *song* and *suffering*. We take the suffering seriously because deadliness sets in when we allow ourselves to become dupes of nostalgia and wishful thinking. We take singing seriously because, in the end, cynicism is a greater lie even than sentimentality.

Heaney tells of an evening in Belfast in 1972 when he and a friend, the singer David Hammond, were planning to make a recording together of songs and poems. It promised to be a joyful evening of music and poetry. They were in an expansive and happy mood. But violence was in the air. Their plans were interrupted by the sound of explosions and later by the sirens of fire engines and ambulances. Finally there came the news of the injured. It was then that they aborted their plans to make a recording. Heaney writes, "The very notion of beginning to sing at that moment when others were beginning to suffer seemed like an offence against their suffering."

Seamus Heaney and David Hammond experienced the tension between "art" and "life," between what Heaney calls song and suffering. Is song a betrayal of suffering? Can catastrophe ever be turned into art? Is all our enjoyment of life a matter of fiddling while Rome burns? As I plunge my fork into some poached salmon, or as I am about to get carried away by *La Bohème,* must someone always remind me of the suffering of humanity? Is there no legitimate way for me to enjoy the world, given what the world is like? This line of questioning leads to nothing but resentment and despair.

There is no reason why the joyful affirmation of the good things of life, including music and poetry, should ever constitute an affront to life. Telling the truth about the human situation requires both the reductionist's eye for the sake of demystification (when it is called for) and the priestly perspective on the sacred and joyful. Ministry has something to do with struggling to tell the whole truth.

I have always been amazed by the way people can sing even in the midst of great suffering. The resilience of the Latin culture, for example, with regard to human suffering is astonishing. The literature and the music are studies in contrasts between suffering and singing, sacrifice and delight. Some people are able to sing in the midst of terrible suffering. They also have the ability to see clearly the importance of our primary relationships, to the extended family of humanity and to God. The peoples of Latin America are possessed of a rootedness that many of us in North America and northern Europe envy. A friend who works with poor people in Central America feels assured that she will be cared for when she is sick and when she gets old. She can enjoy no such assurance in the United States.

Of course, we can admire another culture without idealizing it. Woundedness is present in the Latin culture too. But it has a crazy sense of the transcendent. It refuses to be reduced and seen only through the prism of its pain. It knows about powerlessness and ignorance from a spiritual point of view. It knows about not being in control of life. We in the "developed" world can't understand why everything doesn't collapse in Latin America. We like to have a grip on things. We want the kind of reality one can manufacture and sell.

Singing Our Way Through Suffering

Human beings require experiences of ecstasy. We need experiences that will take us out of ourselves; and if true and life-bearing experiences aren't available to us, we will manufacture some. In the "developed" world we are masters at false transcendence. We specialize in theme-park spirituality. We can guarantee ecstasy without risk. But we in fact produce an addictive society that knows little or nothing about singing and suffering as they relate to the holy and the sacred.

One great model of song and suffering is Saint John of the Cross. Born in 1542 in Castile, Spain, he became one of the great Carmelite friar-reformers. The Carmelites owed their inspiration to the Old Testament prophet Elijah, whose wild and energetic presence on Mount Carmel and subsequent ascent into heaven in a fiery chariot have had a great impact on the religious imagination. John's passionate life and hard death have all the ingredients of ministry writ large, the desire to create and to serve, the sinning and cruelty of communities, the bizarre behavior of human beings, and the hint of glory.

John of the Cross was a poet of paradoxes. He lived for long periods of his life in solitude, yet his theme was union with God and with all things. He thought of prayer as the simple act of considering God the most beautiful creator of beauty. John was taken up by sheer wonder. He needed solitude to see the wonder, and yet the wonder drew him more and more deeply into communion and community. He also sought freedom from the senses, yet his poetry is deeply erotic. One key word in his poetry is *arrobamiento,* "rapture." "There he gave me his breast, / There he taught me a most delicious science / And I gave him myself without reserve."

The questions I have to ask myself are, "Am I open to experiences that might place me in a position of powerlessness? Am I open to the transcendent? Am I open to ecstasy?" Here is a monastic using the imagery of sexuality and saying in effect, "Human beings cannot help but love! Let yourself go!"

163

John of the Cross was a mystic who was also a reformer. He changed his world by looking into the darkness to find fire, by searching for and finding comfort in what he did not and could not know by means of intellect alone, and by discovering that it was this "ignorance" that gave him hope in his knowing. He withdrew from the world to be close to God, yet the doorway to God was through the wonder of nature and human love. He was blinded into a loving darkness by the brightness of the Sun. What he saw left him stunned and stammering. His response to the wonder of the dazzling darkness was to write love poems. He wrote his greatest ones in the midst of terrible suffering. He was tortured and crippled by his accusers (members of his own community!), yet he wrote joyfully and without rancor. He was only severe against himself. He bore no resentment.

John of the Cross wrote at a time of immense upheaval in his own community. The authorities wanted to stop the reform movement started by Saint Teresa, and at one point, when Teresa had been elected superior of a convent, the provincial burned the ballots. Because John was a friend and supporter of Teresa, he was imprisoned in a closet in the friary in Toledo. It was unlit and too low for him to stand. This little cell was bitter cold in winter, stifling hot in summer.

While John was in prison, he was taken each day to the refectory to eat bread and water and sardine scraps from the floor. He also endured the circular discipline: While John knelt, the monks walked around him hitting him with leather whips. At first they did this every day and then only on Fridays. John's shoulders were so badly injured by the beatings that he was crippled for life. He had no change of clothing for six months and was infested with lice. He was reduced to "poor unaccommodated man—the thing itself."

In the middle of all this suffering and mistreatment, John wrote his greatest love poems. A kind jailer gave him paper and pen, which enabled him to record some of his poems. Other verses he memorized. One night outside his window he heard a popular love song.

> I am dying of love darling, what shall I do?
> Just die then!

It was this that inspired his two great poems, "La Noche Obscura" and "El Cántico Espiritual," the "Dark Night" and the "Spiritual Song." John finally escaped with the help (he was convinced) of the Blessed

Virgin Mary. After a period of success and hard work for the reform movement, he was later exiled on false evidence. He ended his days suffering from fever and terrible ulcers on his legs. The prior of Ubeda, where he was detained, refused to help him and came every day to his cell to insult him. John died on the night of 14 December 1591. He was forty-nine years old. In 1726 he was canonized.

The events after his death were both macabre and bizarre. His admirers fought over his remains. A leg was left in Ubeda, where he died; an arm found its way to Madrid; fingers went to various places; and what was left of him was sent to Segovia. There was an appeal to Rome, and the rest of his limbs were cut off and sent back to Ubeda. His was a life that combined many of the elements of the theater described by Peter Brook, from sublime holiness to grim humor. Such is the paradox of human experience. "San Juan suffered the felicity of mystical dying, the harsh pain of bodily death, and finally a macabre disfigurement . . . a man whose life was marked by torture and rapture, a man who always sought the harsh night, the small cell, the lonely exile, yet saw through the night, was entranced by beauty, and gave himself entirely to *his quest for love and light*."[5]

In the life and death of John of the Cross, the "holy" and the "rough" (in the sense that Brook uses these terms to describe two kinds of theater) collide. Holiness, the bizarre, and the disgusting exist side by side in his story. They coexist in the life of the ordained. John of the Cross described his life as a sort of hunt in the game of love. The minister is a kind of hunter in a special chase. Singing and suffering are its peculiar marks.

To Be Spiritually Illiterate

In spite of all the problems of religion as a social phenomenon, and in spite of our built-in fear of holiness, I am constantly taken by surprise by people who are apparently devoid of a need for ritual and ceremony. They don't seem to need song to get along. They seem to have been able to cut themselves off from the feelings and experiences to which John of the Cross speaks. They cannot translate their experiences of being in love, and of being at their wits' end about it, to their orientation to that boundless mystery we call God.

When it comes to basic matters of faith, many people are functionally illiterate. They cannot "read" their experiences, because they cannot connect them with the song and the suffering that is at their center. They have no song to sing or story to tell. They catch a glimpse at a possible reading on special occasions: at a funeral or at the birth of a baby, at a wedding, at a Thanksgiving dinner, or at a Christmas party. We feel a stab of transcendence when we find ourselves caught up in a piece of music or a sunset or when we visit a place that triggers memories. When there is a death in the family, many people drag up the memory of "religion" and construct a makeshift shelter from the bits and pieces of a barely remembered faith.

In the United States, we have three main choices: Protestant, Catholic, and Jewish. We treat these great traditions not as repositories of singing and suffering but as if they were deposits in a bank. We ignore them most of the time and draw on them in time of need. Many clergy are often little more than spiritual impresarios. Some, it is true, are running a good show. They pack 'em in, but there is little real singing and suffering. The Church is broken up into special-interest groups, cut off from each other: right-to-lifers, gay Catholics, Christian drag racers, and Christian surfers, to name a few. The clergy, if they are not careful, become chaplains for local causes and groups. Then the larger vision is lost. The search for holiness without tradition and the hope for delight without sacrifice are both vain.

Neutralizing the Holy

Peter Brook writes, "It is not the fault of the holy that it has become a middle-class weapon to keep children good."[6] People reject the idea of the holy because their experience of it has been false. We have substituted niceness for holiness in both the theater and the church as a way of neutralizing our reaction to the deep encounter with the holy. We want tame and inoffensive plays and tame and inoffensive liturgy. We get what we pay for. We get the clergy and the actors to suit our taste. We deny the mystery at the heart of ministry, and by so doing we cut ourselves off from vast tracts of human experience. We remain in the shallows of human feeling. We become bored and boring. There is nothing to sing about. Clergy need to find their voice and reclaim their vocation as protest against the debilitating cycle of the stock market and affirm the lost cycle of sacrifice and delight.

Making Contact

A Saint John of the Cross can speak to me across the centuries about singing and suffering. The experience of the flame of God's love was uniquely his, yet it is also mine. Sometimes an actor in a play, with a gesture, a statement, perhaps a private manifestation of loneliness, gives a signal to me through the flames, and contact is made.[7] This is the strain and the glory of making the invisible visible.

Perhaps the task to make the tension between order and anarchy creative is too much for us. Artists and ministers have been broken by it. The singing and the suffering get to be too much. I want more "craziness" in the Church, but it cannot be just any kind of craziness. It has to be the kind of madness that wakes us up and invites us to live and to sing.

We never get it quite right. That is why the life of the ordained minister is characterized by penitence and reconciliation, as well as by singing and suffering. How else do we prepare ourselves for the shock of freedom? How else do we respond to our hunger for the invisible to break out into the visible?

The minister's life is a cycle of song and suffering, sacrifice and delight. And what of the spectators, the audience, the congregation? The questions for them, which are explicit in the actor's performance, in the minister's acting his part, are, Do you want to change? Do you want anything different for yourself, your life, your community? Do you want to sing? If you don't, then you don't need the Church or the theater "to be an aid, a magnifying glass, a searchlight, or a place of confrontation."[8] You don't need opportunities to worship.

Are we so dazzled by power and prestige that we forget our essential fragility, that we are all under mercy? How else can we face the grim truths of existence? Primo Levi wrote, "Willingly or not we come to terms with power forgetting that we are all in the ghetto, that the ghetto is walled in, that outside the ghetto reign the lords of death, and that close by the train is waiting."[9] This is confrontation with the dread that we fear. This is a sign of the suffering of the world. If we are open to it, it can also be the occasion of our transformation. The suffering says, "The world is like this." The song says, "Yes, but it can change."

CHAPTER TWELVE

Making One Family
Out of Strangers

I remember being interviewed for ordination at a selection conference in England in 1959. I was brought face to face with a deep issue of faith that had to do with what I believed about my father. I was asked what seemed a peculiar question about him by an archdeacon, a grandly robed Anglo-Catholic. "I see," he said, reading from my file, "that your father died several years ago. Where is he now?"

I was dumbfounded. My father was a bricklayer. I remember him always coming home late for Sunday dinner, sleepy and full of beer. He never went to church and had little time for religion. I fudged my answer. "I don't know, father," I replied.

"You don't know!" exclaimed the priest in mock surprise. "He was baptized, wasn't he?"

I mumbled, "Yes."

"Then he's with God in heaven."

This question about the whereabouts and status of my dead father set me on a path to discover a generous and daring theology. It wasn't that the unbaptized were in hell (a view that is still horribly alive) but that my father was loved by God. This incident drew me into the arms of an inclusive Catholicity and turned me into a virtual universalist, although I am theologically sophisticated enough to allow for the possibility of someone saying "No!" to God and to love forever. My old dad was in heaven! At least he stood a chance. I didn't realize Christianity, especially in its Anglican form, could be so hospitable and generous as to include someone like my father. I didn't think he'd be allowed in.

The Jesus of my childhood and adolescence, after all, was of a different class. This Jesus was very English, was good at games, well connected, and had studied theology at Oxford. Where would my dad and a million like him be welcome? Not here surely. Yet such is the generosity of God. God has no taste! All are welcome. I very much regret that I allowed the English class system to sour my faith. Such a souring was and is a waste of time and energy. The question about the Church, in the end, is not, Who is in and who is out? but, Who knows and who doesn't?

Being is communion. Reality is community. These are the "open secrets" of Christian ministry. In affirming these, we have begun to give some definition to the work of ministry. As we have seen, the ministry is committed to telling stories and singing songs that have a definite pattern to them, even if they do not belong to one single tradition. We are asking, Is there any corpus of *shared* experience that can help us in our search for a community of trust? How do we escape from the prison of our private self? How are we liberated into community? What role does the minister play?

Two Kinds of Freedom

We court danger both personally and politically by relegating freedom to the private sphere and by making ministers the massagers of privatized egos. Two kinds of freedom are of concern to us: the freedom to make choices and the freedom that comes from knowing that the choice we have made is the correct one. We know more about the first freedom and precious little about the second. We are in a double bind. We have done a great deal politically and personally to expand our range of choices. But we have made the false assumption that we will know what to choose when we are free to do so.

The minister cannot help but be involved with people in their basic choices and the muddle they make of their lives. The right choice is communion with all and community for all. This is foolish if it means "anything goes." Choosing a truly open and inclusive community would be agony for some people. It would be hell.

Because we know only about the first freedom, the freedom to make choices, we are often in conflict with one another. I am your potential enemy. I am someone against whom you had better define and defend yourself. Hence our attraction to despotism, our desire to shake off the loneliness of private choice for the "happiness" of a slave. Ironically we choose private freedom in exchange for public slavery or manipulation. Hence people like the "strong minister" who will relieve them of choice and tell them what to do. The Church becomes a safe excluding community instead of a sacrificial inclusive one.

The Easy Solution of a New Beginning

The agony of modern freedom is accurately expressed by the character Crimond in Iris Murdoch's novel *The Book and the Brotherhood*. Crimond is a Marxist charismatic who believes that only a completely new beginning will save the world. Human beings have to be made over. The situation is so desperate that it demands a new world, peopled by new persons. He is like many ministers I know, angry and frustrated. Crimond's Utopia is a wildly happy place. His is a song about the future, a story about heaven on earth. Meanwhile those of us left, barely conscious of what is promised us, are spiritual cripples, half-persons. We simply haven't a clue about freedom. He exclaims to his friend Gerard, "I don't think you know what freedom means. You imagine it's just economic tinkering plus individual human rights. But you can't have freedom when all social relations are wrong, unjust, irrational—when the body of your society is diseased, deformed—we must clear the ground."[1]

The key phrase for our purposes is "you can't have freedom when all social relations are wrong." He is right, but his solution is to scrap what we have and start again. For human beings there is no such thing as starting again from scratch. We can make a new beginning, but we always build on or are in reaction to the past. The irony is that Crimond's diagnosis of our condition is correct, but his overall vision is distorted. He knows about the sacrifice at the heart of it all, but he hates the very people he would see transformed.

> Can you see this bourgeois democracy changing itself? Come! We've got to see it all . . . we've got to live it all, we've got to suffer it all, we've got to see how *disjointed* it all is. . . . We must think . . . it hurts so, one must make

a shot at the whole thing and that means failing too, not really being able to connect, and not pretending things fit when they don't—and keeping hold of the things that don't fit, keeping them whole and clear in their almost-fittingness—oh God, it's so hard.[2]

Most ministers don't have Crimond's capacity for hard thinking about the nature of freedom. We want things to fit. We want to be happy. We want an easygoing communion. All the distortions of religion and politics spring from our longing for some kind of communion, but for a communion that excludes large numbers of people. We do not want others crowding in and spoiling what we have worked hard to build. The Christian minister, however, is a reminder to everyone of our deep longing for the reconciliation of flesh and spirit, self and other, beyond the frontier of guilt and shame.

Ministry Is Learning to Forgive

As we have seen, reconciliation and forgiveness are the prerequisites for true communion and community. Our shared stories speak to our desire to be freed from guilt and shame. My narcissistic self argues, "With the world as it is, who really wants community? Only a madman would want communion. Only an idiot would be a minister!" But still less do I want the isolation of my sweaty little self. My infantilism yields to a frightening truth (at least frightening to my treacherous and oh-so-clever little ego), that the work of building a saving community cannot happen in the privacy of my little and limited imagination. It has to take shape in cooperation with others. It is going to mean building actual communities, made up of weak and silly people. It is going to mean not only rigorous thinking but also the willingness to let the stranger in, the unpredictable and treacherous stranger. Uncomfortable convictions begin to invade my private world when I want to end my isolation.

If we could accept ourselves as dependent and contingent, we might be able to experience something of the freedom of a Saint Augustine, who knew himself first to be gift: "God's first gift to me is my own fragile self." When we understand that about ourselves, our lives can then be understood as a sheer unmerited and unearned gift, the response to which is one long act of thanksgiving, characterized by sacrifice and delight.

No Community Without God

Why do people persist on this dangerous and inconclusive quest for God? They want to locate him, get a fix on him, which, of course, is a terrible kind of madness. Perhaps that's why some ministers come to grief. We are a constant disappointment because we cannot get a fix on "this unnamed and unsignposted expanse of our consciousness." If we did manage to get a handle on God, we would merely have a construction of our imagination and desire.

Martin Buber tells us that if we try to drop the word *God* altogether and concentrate our energies on building community, we shall not get very far. Dispensing with the word might solve a lot of problems but, as Buber reminds us, "It is the most heavy laden of human words. None has become so soiled, so mutilated. Just for this reason I may not abandon it. Generations of men have laid the burden of their lives upon this word and weighed it to the ground; it lies in the dust and bears their whole burden. . . . But we may not give it up."[3] We may not give it up because we may not give up on ourselves. The question of God's presence in the world always concerns the possibility of human community. When God is left out of the picture (eclipsed, as Buber would say), when God is absent from the world, there is the absence of relation, of human community.[4] There is no room for the stranger, and, at various moments of our lives, we are all strangers.

Standing in Two Places at Once

We are terrified of having a point of view (a definite story or song) because the supreme virtue of our age is to see everything as relative. Such a view is, in fact, nonsensical. It is hard for us to take sides, but a point of view is unavoidable. Without it I am nobody. I have no form. I have no character. The recovery of God-talk will involve our coming to terms with our moral laziness in building a community of trust and our neurotic need to put the things that matter to us (possessions and ideas) into a private place where no one else can get at them.

Is there any reason (apart from what I can make from the sow's ear of my contradictory feelings) why I should bother about you? I cannot find any reason inside myself. But I can find abundant reasons if I listen to the stories and songs that come to me from the long stream of human experience. We need to initiate a conversation with our past. We need to learn a few stories and dig up some old songs. What we want is something more down to earth than arguments and rationalizations. We want stories, traditions, and songs that "actually create persons whose nature is such that certain things count without question as reasons, justifications and criticisms of conduct for them."[5]

Some want to withdraw from the world because "it would be better to have confident agreement in principle among the members of a narrower group with a common formation than endless disagreement among everybody." I think we have to have both. We have to maintain the songlines, the dream-tracks, of our own tradition but to realize that in the end there is only one Song with infinite variations and harmonies.

As a priest, I believe I am called to stand in two places at once, at the center of a particular story-telling tradition and at its edge. We would be no good to anyone if we lost our own music, but we would be tone-deaf if we refused to listen to the music of others. The basic point is this: To be human we have to belong to a community. You cannot say you are without reference to a community, to a community capable of including the stranger.

The Four Secrets

We have four secrets of ministry for making a community out of strangers and false friends:

- Being is communion.
- Reality is community.
- Reconciliation and forgiveness are freely offered.
- Thanksgiving is the response to the sheer giftedness of life.

A totally private world is hell. Our belief that we can find meaning in private existence without a shared view of the world and its ultimate purpose leads to a narcissistic dead end. Perhaps we should be more astonished by the fact that individuals manage, in both the silence and the babble, to find sufficient meaning and purpose than by the spiritual emptiness of the times.[6]

Why, then, do I long for conversation among the traditions, for an exchange of stories, for the sharing of dreams? Because the problems that confront us are so colossal that the old rhetoric of the Right and the Left, the conservative and the liberal, won't do anymore. We need a common language of the good that is not held captive to either the revolutionary or the reactionary, either religiously or politically.

Right-Wing Clergy and Left-Wing Ministers

All this may seem a long way from our creating a community of compassion, of making a family out of strangers and false friends. Before we can approach this issue, we will have to make some decision with regard to the kind of world we live in and the actual status of the stories we like to tell. Let us take a look at the world as it is seen through the eyes of the "Left" and the "Right."

One of my heroes is John Henry Newman, who was attacked for being a reactionary in the first half of his life and for being a liberal in the second. Meriol Trevor, in the second volume of her biography of Newman, writes of the England of the 1860s:

> To many the tension seemed then, and seems now, to be between two views only: the progressive or revolutionary, and the traditional or reactionary. It is because Newman from the beginning proposed a third to this antagonistic duo and because all through his life he was the representative of a view at once apocalyptic and developmental, which combined tradition with intellectual enquiry, that his influence increased rather than diminished as the century went on and more and more people were forced to face fundamental questions of the meaning and value of human life.[7]

Liberalism has a bad name because of its failure to be rooted in tradition. The word *liberal* needs as much rehabilitation as the word *God*. The new-style "liberal" lives in a radically different world from mine. Hers is a "modern" world of the private imagination. It's one where people behave badly only because of ignorance. They don't sin. They are just bad at moral arithmetic. It's a world of "life-style enclaves" rather than of communities. It is at once rationalistic and crazy. It is a world dominated by a scientific fundamentalism as rigid and as intransigent as its biblical twin.

This kind of liberal is a "modern man" who must feel justified at all costs. He has a view of the past that assumes that our ancestors were all unenlightened troglodytes. They did their best, of course, given what they knew, but we know better. In this so-called liberal world "facts" are confused with "values." He has a high time relativizing and caricaturing the past, but he doesn't see the necessity of being as critical and cautious with regard to the present. His time is now. The past is merely a collection of cautionary tales about human folly and prejudice. The future is mistily irrelevant.

My fear is that a generation brought up on this short-term view will have hell to pay later on because of its blindness to the boundless mystery. Liberals of this sort need no ministers.

Yet rigid conservatism is no better. It too is the enemy of the conversation for building an inclusive community of trust in which the stranger, the poor, the oppressed are welcome. It has no concept of the various levels of truth. Truths never change, conservatives say. That may be so, but the rigid conservative cannot make the distinction between truth and our inadequate formulations of it. I know many ministers who cannot make the distinction. For them, one either believes in a univocal understanding of the tradition or has sold out.

Dwelling In and Breaking Out

The rigid conservative and equally rigid liberal views need each other. They are represented by two distinct ways of dealing with reality, described as *dwelling in* and *breaking out*. We need to learn what it is to dwell in and break out of ideas and concepts. Stories teach us how and when to dwell in or break out.

Michael Polanyi writes about the way a too tightly held view of reality leads to stagnation, especially when we claim that our approximations to the truth are final answers. We end up with a dry dogmatism and loss of meaning and a community that is defensive and rigid.

> When we *dwell in* our convictions about the world with passion—neither merely observing from a distance nor seeking total control, but rather living in them (as we dwell in our bodies)—it becomes possible for new insight to occur, for innovative revelation to happen. . . . In those times we *break out* of the framework in which we have been dwelling . . . to new discovery. It is only by *dwelling in* that *breaking out* becomes possible.[8]

We find the breaking out side of the equation in the open and unfinished character of stories that invite us to enter into conversation with them. That is why we can read them over and over again and never exhaust their meaning. They leave room for the new and are important to communities that define themselves as being willing to make room for the stranger.

Most of us, however, want to have things figured out. We want to know if Anna Karenina is the victim of a narrow-minded tyrant or if, on the contrary, Karenin is the victim of an immoral woman. Is Hamlet a procrastinating coward or a brave victim of circumstances? Milan Kundera writes that the novel may be "the territory where no one possesses the truth, neither Anna nor Karenin, but where everyone has the right to be understood, both Anna and Karenin."[9] That is why the novel is so hated by totalitarian regimes, and why it seems to have less and less of a place in a consumer culture that is growing daily more devoted to what can be assimilated without effort.

For me the novel, above every other form today, feeds the much-needed public conversation by refusing to give easy and slick answers. "All great works (precisely because they are great) contain something unachieved." Our life is also a great work, and yet it is something unachieved. Hence our need for each other, our need for community, our need for communion.

Jobs to Be Done Among Strangers

One of the hardest things to bear as a minister is the false view people (both within and outside the Church) have of Christianity. Many of my friends outside the Church see it as a corrupt and corrupting influence. They take the point of view of Crimond, the angry Marxist in Iris Murdoch's novel *The Book and the Brotherhood*. Crimond has an ongoing quarrel with Christianity, which he sees as the Cult of the Individual (which is the last thing it is). "We are fat with false morality and inwardness and authenticity and decayed Christianity. . . . It's the final orgy, the last stand of the so-called incarnate individual, who has withered into a little knot of egoism, even the concept stinks. It's the end of civilization which gloats over personal adventures."[10] This, of course, is a travesty of Christianity, but one that the clergy are partly responsible for constructing, all inwardness and individualism.

Jenkin is the Christ figure in the novel. He is the one character free of ideology. Jenkin has an easy, natural contemplative presence. He knows the art of the conversation and is committed to the walkabout. He is a walker and is able to imagine and enjoy the otherness of others, their separateness and individuality. He is open to the stranger. For him there is no supernatural "elsewhere." There is only "now," but it's a now full of generous possibility. He is present in the world in a special way. Gerard, his friend, is always wrapped "in the great dark cloak of his thoughts," whereas Jenkin walked his way through "a great collection or exhibition of little events or encounters. Trees, for instance, an immense variety of dogs whose gentle soft friendly eyes met his with intelligence, rubbish tips containing an amazing variety of things which people threw away, some of which Jenkin would take home and cherish . . . "[11]

Iris Murdoch has Jenkin shed the gentle and loving religion of his parents. The irony is that in truth he does not shed it. He lives it. "He could not believe in a supernatural elsewhere or imagine the risen Lord except in anguish. He found equally alien the (as he saw it) quasi-mystical, pseudo-mystical, Platonic perfectionism which was Gerard's substitute for religious belief. Yet he retained . . . a kind of absolutism, not about any special human task or pilgrimage, but just about jobs to be done among strangers."[12] That last is the key phrase—"jobs to be done among strangers." Jenkin instinctively knew the rules of the "priestly" life. He was in the world in such a way that his presence was humane and life bearing. He knew that the stranger was his brother. He was connected with everyone and everything. In him were the grounds for the building of a community of trust. His friend Gerard was much more self-conscious about his spiritual life than he was. Gerard talked egotistically about "destroying his ego," whereas "Jenkin quite liked his, he needed it, he never worried too much, he hoped to do better."[13]

Jenkin saw the heroes of our time as the "dissidents, protesters, people alone in cells, anonymous helpers, unknown truth-tellers." He did not aspire to be one, "but he wanted to be somehow near them." His orientation was simple and direct. He wouldn't have called it boundless mystery, but his direct awareness of and presence to others suggested that he was deeply aware of "the other" in his life.

> Nothing mattered much except easing pain, except individuals and their histories. But what did that mean for him . . . ? Even his Liberation Theology

was romantic, consisting merely of a popular picture of Christ as the Saviour of the poor, of the left-behinds, of the disappeareds. Though sometimes he also thought, could that just not be theology after all, not the learned tinkering of demythologising bishops, but theology broken, smashed by the sudden realisable and realised horror of the world?[14]

Jenkin was a "priestly" man. Those of us who are ordained have much to learn from him and from his effect on his friend Gerard. Gerard experiences his own weakness in the presence of Jenkin's simplicity. He was palpably threatened by Jenkin's knowledge of the songlines or the aboriginal dream-tracks that hold the world together. Jenkin made Gerard look at his powerlessness and ignorance. Perhaps that's why he had to die. The minister is often the instrument by which people are introduced to their powerlessness and ignorance. Gerard "had exchanged his power for an infinite vulnerability."[15] Ministry is about such an exchange—the exchange of one kind of power for that of an infinite vulnerability.

In the face of all this, perhaps all I can do is to retreat into the little world of my ministry in my denomination and muddle along and do my best. Jenkin's way won't do in the end because he fails to see the value of an actual fallible and often silly institution—the Church. He fails to move beyond the individual to the community.

The image of a community sharing stories and breaking bread means a great deal to me. It requires a tradition, an organization, an institution. To be centered in story and bread means experiencing the world as both a guest and a host. Its principle is sharing. It makes clear the sacredness of society, the social body of the community. That is why some of us are notoriously inclusive and have trouble making clear boundaries for the Church. When the Church breaks bread, it is saying we live in and for one another.

That is why I find worship both essential and difficult: essential because it is constitutive of my humanity; difficult because it means that I cannot be me without you. I have to make room for the stranger. The Church, for all its faults, is committed to making a community out of strangers and even of false friends.

The Needs of Strangers

Michael Ignatieff gives us some clues about communion in his *The Needs of Strangers*.[16] We take certain needs for granted—income, food, clothing, shelter, medical care. But we need more than survival. We need love, belonging, dignity—priestly things. Our genius, alas, lies "in respecting individuals' rights while demeaning them as persons." We know that money can't buy the respect, love, and honor we need. Still less can merely invoking our so-called rights guarantee we'll receive what we think we are owed. That is why "any decent society requires a public discourse about the needs of the human person."[17] We need a language of the good as well as of rights because many acts of love, kindness, and virtue cannot be spelled out as legal civil obligations. You cannot make me love and honor you. I cannot make you love me.

What then do we have in common? One language we have in common is the language of need. Ignatieff uses Shakespeare's play *King Lear* as a prism through which to look at basic human need. Lear's outburst "Oh, reason not the need" (II. iv) is what a person cries when he or she is cornered and trapped by a society that demands reasons for acting morally. When Goneril asks the old man the devastating question about the number of knights in his retinue, "What need you of five-and-twenty, ten or five," she hits at the core of her father's soul.

At last the proud and foolish old man has to do something he hasn't done before: he has to use the language of need. Imagine a situation when you are in need and the response is, "Why? Give me a reason! Tell me why I should help you!" With Goneril's question, Lear is brought face to face with the brutal simplicities of the merciless. The clue to Lear's character is given in the first scene of act I. "'Tis the infirmity of his age; yet he hath ever but slenderly know himself." Lear was totally unprepared for the collapse of his world.

Ignatieff's point is that *Lear* is a play "that sets out to show us why we must take the needs of others on trust. Shakespeare shows us "how murderous and pitiless the world can become without such trust." What should the relationship between the powerful and the powerless be? Surely the one thing they have in common is need. The "nightmare of the powerless is that one day they will make their claim and the powerful will demand a reason, one day the look of entreaty will be met with the unknowing stare of force."[18] I need you to trust me when I tell you my needs. The Church, above all, is the community of such trust, and we are its ministers.

Hence the return to the theme of trust and trustworthiness as being the heart of building a community in which communion is possible. Our needs provide us with knowledge that we cannot learn by any way other than suffering and sacrifice.

Isn't the minister compelled to proclaim and celebrate this basic human solidarity, a solidarity in need? What is it I find I need? "The chance to understand and be understood, to love and be loved, to forgive and be forgiven."[19] Are not these common needs? How can we wake up to them and to each other?

"And the Word Became Flesh and Dwelt Among Us"

The minister or priest is the servant of the Word, and "unspoken common ground is the very stuff of human connection."[20] The minister is the one ordained (ordered) to speak about the things that tend to remain unspoken. What is it that puts our humanity to the test? It is our poor weak flesh we share and nothing else, and we share it with everyone.

This reminds me of a key line in the Christian Story: "And the Word became *flesh* and dwelt among us!" Entertain this as a dogma about what dwells in *your* flesh. Perhaps we ministers, in particular, need to begin with the lowest common denominator of our fleshliness before we can see our flesh in all its glory and possibility. None of us, after all, is immune from common bestiality. Our education in compassion is costly. "We never know a thing till we have paid to know it, never know how much is enough until we have had much less than enough, never know what we need until we have been dispossessed." The road back to being human leads through the land of tragedy.[21] Sacrifice is at the heart of the Church as it seeks to make a family out of strangers.

I come full circle. To be truly human is a matter of trust. The ministers of Christ are committed to being close to their own powerlessness, so that the sharing of power with the stranger isn't a threat. We confer our humanity on one another. It is a gift. We exist on this planet as one another's guests. Life is communion.

In our search for communion and community, we cannot help but bump into God. God's first gift to us is our own fragile self. Our ministry (ordained or not) is to return the gift for the making of a family out of strangers.

Ministry: Playing with God and Befriending the Universe

Everyone is born a priest. Life is marked by a cycle of sacrifice and delight. Some people seem to be familiar with the cycle. Others find that it comes to the surface once or twice in a lifetime. A few have never known it.

The Terrible Gift

A story in the book of Lie Zi (third century B.C.E.) tells of a man who possessed a terrible gift. He could identify thieves on sight. All he had to do was look at a certain spot between the eye and the brow and he would know whether or not that person was a thief. The emperor was duly impressed and naturally gave the man an important position in the ministry of justice. The thieves got wind of the appointment and banded together and assassinated him before he could take office. "For this reason clear-sighted people were generally considered cripples, bound to come to a bad end."[1]

We will always need people willing to take the risk of ministry for the sake of making the world anew. D. H. Lawrence wrote in his novel

Kangaroo that some people "have to be bombs, to explode and make breaches in the walls that shut life in."[2] The challenge of ministry is the challenge to change our lives.

How do we bear the burden of ministry, whether ordained or not? It is a gift. Even if we betray it, it is still a gift. In classic Catholic theology the maxim is "Peter baptizes, Christ baptizes. Even Judas baptizes, yet still Christ baptizes."

I remember two priests from my early days in my ministry. They were about my age, and both are now dead. One died of a terrible wasting disease, the other took his own life. The former was a meticulous and fussy black-suited Anglo-Catholic. He was physically contorted, smoked incessantly and affectedly, and was theologically opinionated. He celebrated Mass as if nothing had changed in the Church since the Counter-Reformation. We all loved him. He had the ability to laugh at himself, and, for all his affectation, what made him tick was love. The other priest's suicide took us all by surprise. He was shy yet naturally affectionate, a man with a fine mind and a caring spirit. He too was rigid in his theology but broad in his pastoral caring. I carry these two priests with me in my prayers. They were my friends, and I know what ministry cost them.

Our Weaknesses Are Part of God's Plan

There is a "minister" in everyone. The secrets of ministry well up in the human spirit when you want to tell a story or sing a song. They bubble over when you want to have a celebration. They frighten you when you come up against your sense of powerlessness and ignorance. They lure you into a cycle of sacrifice and delight. Above all, the secrets of ministry reveal to us that we are blessed and that we are to bless in return.

Richard Bolles, a wonderful priest who has influenced many people through the ministry of his best-selling book *What Color Is Your Parachute?* preached a sermon for the installation of a pastor in which he made the following comments: "We are a people whose weaknesses are part of God's plan. God neither creates that weakness, nor ordains it, but He does have a plan for how to deal with it when it inevitably appears.

The plan is: forgiveness." The plan is forgiveness. It is this that will remake the world. The task of the priest (ordained or not) is to be a bearer of the healing word of forgiveness by being a teller of tales and a breaker of bread.

In the end, ministry is deceptively simple. We tend not to trust the simplicity at the heart of religion, that we were made by love and for love. There is the wonderful humility of faith, being grounded in the earth (*humus*), which gives us a sense of proportion, the opposite of self-importance. Faith is the ability, once in a while, to be lovingly aimless, instead of being on the treadmill of goals and schemes. Faith is the grace not to take ourselves too seriously. It sounds wonderful. But it's very hard to be genuinely simple and trusting. Yet this is the message of the gospel of which we are ministers. We are told that we can keep all the Commandments simply by loving God and by loving our neighbor. But we either despise or distrust simplicity or we opt for a false and dangerous kind of simplification.

There is, after all, a resentful simplicity in the face of a chaotic and disordered world. The Nazis had an elegantly simple view of the universe. The extermination of millions of people was a simple final solution. Evil has a terrible simplicity about it. One July Fourth I listened on public radio to a spokeswoman for the Revolutionary Communist party. She had an elegant solution to our problems as a nation—armed insurrection. A new world would be ushered in once a few of us had been wiped out. We love the simple solution that bypasses the brain. We choose not to notice the gap between human aspiration and human behavior.

The Gift of Simplicity
Is the Work of a Lifetime

I love the words of Jesus in the Gospel, "Come to me, all who labor and are heavy laden, and I will give you rest." But the gap between what I am and what I want to be seems infinite. One of the great students of Buddhism reiterated for a disciple the wisdom of the Buddha. "Always do good. Never do evil. Keep your mind pure." And the impatient response was "I knew that when I was three years old! Any fool knows that!" The reply? "Yes, and a three year old may know it, but even an eighty year old man can't put it into practice." It is one thing to understand. It is quite another to receive it like a little child.

I am healed by the brilliance of Saint Paul's diagnosis of the basic human problem of the divided heart—"I know what I ought to do, why then don't I do it? I find it to be a law, that when I want to do right, evil lies close at hand, wretched man that I am" (Rom. 7:19–24). I struggle with two laws inside me: one of flesh and one of the Spirit. They get me into trouble. Saint Paul is concerned with the transformation of consciousness.

When we hear the word *flesh,* we think it refers to the false battle between the body and the spirit. Saint Paul isn't talking about flesh in that sense. He's talking about the law of short-term goals, the law of narrow, mean-spirited vision that sees only the immediate. Paul is brilliant, because he acknowledges that there is no way out of this bind. He knows that we need a savior. He speaks directly to the torments of the religiously sensitive, to that which agitates our memory and our imagination.

We try to reduce the problem, to slay the intractable mystery at the heart of every human being. We simplify in order to destroy. We slay what we should love. We repress and deny what loves us. We push away the mystery inside us. We fight it instead of learning what it is trying to teach us.

The simplicity of the gospel brings me to the end of my rope. "I thank thee Father, Lord of heaven and earth, that thou didst hide these things from the wise and understanding and didst reveal them unto babes" (Matt. 11:25, RSV). The gospel reveals the humility of God. "Your king comes to you triumphant and glorious, humble and riding on a donkey" (Matt. 21:5). This is the God we claim to worship.

The Yoke of Christ

I wonder what burden we ministers need to set aside to take on the easy yoke of Christ. What are we carrying around right now that needs to be left behind? I carry around something very much common in the latter part of the twentieth century—I carry around myself. In our age each person's self has become his or her principal burden. We are caught in a trap. To know oneself is not meant to be an end in itself. It is meant to be the instrument through which we know others in the world.

In my own need for salvation, I want that hall of mirrors in which I live to be smashed. I need simple companionship to break through those intense moments of loneliness when I am constantly worrying about myself. What weighs us down? What is the enemy of our delight? What does it take for us to give up the poisonous burden of our fear and contempt for others, a contempt that rots the soul?

Befriending the Universe

The invitation to ministry is simple. It is to become a child again. We become a child by being friendly with the universe. Huston Smith reports a conversation with an Asian friend about the climbing of Mount Everest. The phrase commonly used in the West to describe the feat was "the conquest of Everest." Smith's Asian friend commented, "In the East we would put matters differently. We would speak of *befriending* Everest."

What a shift of attitude there is from conquest to befriending! What about the befriending of yourself? Have we ever thought of befriending ourselves instead of conquering ourselves? Ministry is the simple vocation of befriending the universe. The shift from conquest to befriending is simple, a small shift but a key one.

Ministry relies on our willingness to become a child, to learn to play again. Enjoy the fact that you are unnecessary! "Thank God your being is unnecessary!" wrote W. H. Auden to his godson. Thank God you're not God! All important things are unnecessary. Friendship is unnecessary, philosophy is unnecessary, art is unnecessary, the whole universe is unnecessary. Since this is so, what is it that gives value to survival? Surely it is the ministry of befriending each other and befriending the universe.

Skills for Ministry

Playfulness and friendliness are two important skills for ministry. These qualities sound lame and sentimental unless we are able to see the passion and sacrifice behind them. The stories we tell and the sacraments we celebrate teach us how to deepen these skills.

Rowan Williams writes of the power of tradition (story telling and bread breaking) to teach us the needed skills for living.[3] He gives us three ways of responding and reacting to things as if the Love Story were true. His three "as ifs" have to do with the skill of being a creature, the skill of being a redeemed creature, and the skill of being a citizen of God's Kingdom.

The skill of being a creature is simply learning what it is to live "as if our existence depended completely on gratuitous generosity." The art of ministry is grounded in the generosity of God.

The skill of being a redeemed creature is a matter of learning "to live as if our failures and betrayals could never extinguish the commitment of God to us and the capacity of God to make something of us." The art of ministry is grounded in the belief that God calls us to be agents of the divine delight. God entrusts us with "the job of witnessing to and diffusing the generosity on which all things depend."

The skill of being a citizen of God's Kingdom is a matter of learning "to live as if we could not move towards God without the gift of one another." I cannot be truly healed and free without the healing and freedom of all.

Playing with God

These three "as ifs" structure the "game" of faith. The game requires a sense of playfulness if we are to experience the healing and wholeness promised to all. We go to church to play with God. Something vital is lost if there is no playfulness in ministry. The play can be serious. There are tears as well as laughter, but it is still play. Worship is a party, with plenty of bread and wine.

The poet Elizabeth Jennings wrote about the delight at the center. The enjoyment of the world depends on those who know what it is for. People are not to be used. Ministry is about gift.

> The world's for delight and each of us
> Is a joy whether in or out of love.
> "No one must ever be used for use,"
> Was what I was thinking of.[4]

The Irish saint, Brigid, the founder of Kildaire, saw life as a feast of befriending in terms of gallons of beer in heaven. She writes, "I should like a great lake of ale, for the king of Kings. I should like the angels of heaven to be drinking through time eternal. I should like excellent meats of belief and pure piety. Barrels of peace. Vessels of love. Cellars of mercy. I should like cheerfulness to be in their drinking. I should like Jesus to be there among them. I should like the people of Heaven, the poor, to be gathered around us from all parts. That's what I would like." We are all befriended. We're here to befriend others. Ministry is an invitation to play—to play with God and with each other.

Notes

PREFACE

1. Raimundo Panikkar, *The Vedic Experience* (Berkeley: Univ. of California Press, 1977), 98.

CHAPTER ONE: BROKEN HUMANITY

1. Alec Guinness, *Blessings in Disguise* (London: Fontana/Collins, 1986), 74.

2. Iris Murdoch, *The Message to the Planet* (London: Chatto & Windus, 1989), 561.

3. Jean Sulivan, *Morning Light* (Mahwah, NJ: Paulist Press, 1989). Jean Sulivan (1913–1980) was a French priest, novelist, and essayist.

4. Herbert Kelly to the Society of the Sacred Mission, 4 October 1917. In a letter to Father Timothy Nakamura, 22 April 1922, he commented: "What is Catholic must be simple and common. But it must also be scholarly, it must be social as well as individual. It must be modern as well as old and orthodox. . . . If you make Catholic truth a very small thing, so you can say:—'Oh, this is Catholicity,' God will laugh at you."

5. James Hillman, *A Blue Fire,* ed. Thomas Moore (New York: Harper & Row, 1989), 284.

6. Margaret Drabble, *The Radiant Way* (New York: Ivy Books [Ballantine], 1987), 69.

CHAPTER TWO: DARING TO BE ORDAINED

1. Monica Furlong, *Zen Effects: The Life of Alan Watts* (London: Hodder, 1984), 84–85.

2. Francis MacManus, *The Greatest of These* (Cork, Ireland: Mercier Press, 1943), 73.

3. Marjorie Casebier McCoy with Charles McCoy, *Frederick Buechner: Novelist and Theologian of the Lost and Found* (San Francisco: Harper & Row, 1988), see 114–15.

4. McCoy and McCoy, *Frederick Buechner,* 114–15.

5. Paraphrased from Karl Rahner's *Servants of the Lord* (New York: Herder & Herder, 1968), 111–12.

6. Jean Sulivan, *Morning Light* (Mahwah, NJ: Paulist Press, 1989), 23.

7. Chaucer's *Canterbury Tales* (Goghill version). See also Nicolson's rendering of the last line, "A shitty shepherd shepherding clean sheep."

8. André Malraux, *Anti-Memoirs* (New York: Holt, Rinehart & Winston, 1968), 103.

9. A. N. Wilson, *How Can We Know? An Essay on the Christian Religion* (New York: Athenaeum, 1985), see 2–3.

10. MacManus, *The Greatest of These,* 62.

CHAPTER THREE: THE MINISTER—GOD'S WOUNDED FOOL

1. Stanza 2:16.

2. Thomas Maeder, "Wounded Healers," *Atlantic Monthly,* January 1989, 37ff.

3. Maeder, "Wounded Healers," 41.

4. Maeder, "Wounded Healers," 42.

5. Robertson Davies, *The Lyre of Orpheus* (New York: Viking, 1989), 295ff.

6. Davies, *The Lyre of Orpheus,* 298.

7. Maeder, "Wounded Healers," 42.

8. See for this and the remarks above, "Demoralizing the Clergy," *Religion and Society Report* 6, 4 (The Rockford Institute, Deerfield, IL, April 1989), 3–5.

9. Robert Coles, *Harvard Diary: Reflections on the Sacred and Secular* (New York: Crossroad), 10–11.

10. Coles, *Harvard Diary,* 11.

11. Oliver Sacks, "The Revolution of the Deaf," *New York Review of Books,* 2 June 1988, 234.

12. See Richard Davenport-Hines, "Blaming the Ill," *Times Literary Supplement,* 29 April–5 May 1988, 453ff., reviewing two books about tuberculosis in Britain: F. B. Smith's *The Retreat of Tuberculosis 1850–1950* and Linda Bryden's *Below the Magic Mountain.*

13. MacManus, *The Greatest of These* (Cork, Ireland: Mercier Press, 1943), 51.

CHAPTER FOUR: NURTURING THE BROKEN MINISTER

1. J. F. Powers, *Wheat That Springeth Green* (New York: Alfred A. Knopf, 1988), 76.

2. Peter Brook, *The Empty Space* (London: Pelican, 1972), 35.

3. *Religion and Society Report* 6, 4 (The Rockford Institute, Deerfield, IL, April 1989).

4. See J. F. Powers's novels and commentary by Dan Wakefield in the *New York Times Book Review*. "Mr. Powers' religious vision is not the dark and bloody ground of O'Connor's Christianity, but rather the gray, twilight landscape of a once-bright but fading faith." Quoted in *Religion and Society Report,* April 1989.

5. Powers, *Wheat That Springeth Green,* 69.

6. *Religion and Society Report,* 36–37.

7. Zygmunt Bauman, "Living with Indeterminacy," *Times Literary Supplement,* 11–17 May 1990, 501.

8. Leonard I. Sweet, "Straddling Modernism and Postmodernism," *Theology Today,* July 1990, 164.

9. Powers, *Wheat That Springeth Green,* 145.

10. Powers, *Wheat That Springeth Green,* 176.

11. Powers, *Wheat That Springeth Green,* 198.

12. The Alban Institute, 4125 Nebraska Ave., NW, Washington, DC 20016.

13. Powers, *Wheat That Springeth Green,* 105.

14. Liam Hudson, "Facilitations," *Times Literary Supplement,* 6–12 July 1990, 723.

15. Hudson, "Facilitations," 723.

16. Hudson, "Facilitations," 723.

17. Roger Walsh, *The Spirit of Shamanism* (Los Angeles: Jeremy Tarcher, 1990), 5.

18. Walsh, *The Spirit of Shamanism,* 6.

19. Walsh, *The Spirit of Shamanism,* 23.

20. See R. S. De Ropp, *The Master Game.* Quoted in Walsh, *The Spirit of Shamanism,* 25.

21. From *The Farther Reaches of Human Nature.* Quoted in Walsh, *The Spirit of Shamanism,* 29.

22. Quoted in Walsh, *The Spirit of Shamanism,* 54.

23. Walsh, *The Spirit of Shamanism,* 262–63.

24. Richard Gilbert, director of Pastoral Care, Porter Memorial Hospital, Valparaiso, IN. Privately distributed.

25. MacManus, *The Greatest of These* (Cork, Ireland: Mercier Press [1943] 1963), 73.

26. Georges Bernanos, "Diary of a Country Priest," *Journal d'un Curé de Campagne* (Paris: Plon, 1936).

CHAPTER FIVE: THE CONTEXT OF MINISTRY

1. See Robert Bellah et al., *Habits of the Heart* (Berkeley: Univ. of California Press, 1985).

2. Jean Sulivan, *Morning Light* (Mahwah, NJ: Paulist Press, 1979), 176.

3. Mark Helprin, in *Visionary San Francisco* (San Francisco: Museum of Modern Art, 1990).

4. Helprin, *Visionary San Francisco.*

5. "Is Windsordom Worth It?" A review of Christopher Hitchens, "The Monarchy," in *Times Literary Supplement,* 16–22 March 1990, 271.

6. See Philip Cushman, "Why the Self Is Empty," *American Psychologist,* May 1990, 599ff.

7. Cushman, "Why the Self Is Empty."

8. Cushman, "Why the Self Is Empty," 600.

9. Cushman, "Why the Self Is Empty," 600.

10. Robert J. Egan, S.J., "Contemplation in the Context of Culture," unpub. 1990.

11. Egan, "Contemplation."

12. See *America in Perspective,* Oxford Analytica (Boston: Houghton Mifflin, 1986).

13. *America in Perspective,* 116.

14. *America in Perspective,* 117.

15. *America in Perspective,* 119–20.

16. See Eugen Weber's review of Daniel Pick's *Faces of Degeneration: European Disorder c. 1848–c. 1918* (Cambridge Univ. Press), in *Times Literary Supplement,* 30 March–5 April 1990, 336.

17. *America in Perspective,* 369.

18. See Timothy Garton Ash, "Eastern Europe: The Year of Truth," *New York Review of Books,* 15 February 1990, 17ff.

CHAPTER SIX: THE MINISTER AS STORYTELLER

1. See Walter Brueggemann, "The Preacher, the Text, and the People," in *Theology Today,* October 1990, 237ff.

2. Brueggemann, "The Preacher," 243–44.

3. Brueggemann, "The Preacher," 244.

4. Brueggemann, "The Preacher," 245.

5. Brueggemann, "The Preacher," 245.

6. E. D. Hirsch, *Cultural Literacy: What Every American Needs to Know* (Boston: Houghton Mifflin, 1987).

7. "The Opening of American Minds," *Harpers,* July 1989, 22.

8. Karl Rahner, *The Practice of Faith: A Handbook of Contemporary Spirituality,* ed. Karl Lehman and Albert Raffelt (New York: Crossroad, 1983), 78.

9. A phrase from the Australian novelist Patrick White.

10. Nicholas Lash, *Easter in Ordinary* (Charlottesville: Univ. of Virginia Press, 1988), 10.

11. See Lash, *Easter in Ordinary,* 104.

12. A phrase from Tom Stoppard's play *Jumpers.*

13. Lash, *Easter in Ordinary,* 104.

14. This section and what follows owes a great deal to Peter Berger's essay "The Concept of Mediating Action" in *Confession, Conflict and Community,* ed. Richard Neuhaus (Grand Rapids, MI: William B. Eerdmans, 1986); and to James Turner's essay "Secular Justifications of Truth-Claims: A Historical Sketch" and Berger's essay "Different Gospels: The Social Sources of Apostasy," in *American Apostasy: The Triumph of "Other" Gospels* (Grand Rapids, MI: William B. Eerdmans, 1989).

15. Peter Berger, "The Concept of Mediating Action," *Confession, Conflict and Community.*

16. See George Lindbeck, *The Nature of Doctrine* (Philadelphia: Westminster Press, 1984).

17. Quoted by Karl Menninger, *Whatever Became of Sin?* (New York: Hawthorn Books, 1973), 201–202.

18. See Lash, *Easter in Ordinary,* 201, commenting on Richard Rorty.

19. Lash, *Easter in Ordinary,* 187.

20. The Rev. Richard Maplebeck-Palmer.

21. Quoted by George Steiner in *George Steiner: A Reader* (London: Penguin, 1984), 36. See also my *Passion for Pilgrimage* (San Francisco: Harper & Row, 1989), 169.

22. See Bruce Chatwin, *Songlines* (London: Penguin, 1987).

23. See also *Granta,* no. 21 (London: Penguin, 1987) for excerpts and commentary.

24. See David H. Smith, *Health and Medicine in the Anglican Tradition* (New York: Crossroad, 1986), 12.

25. Lash, *Easter in Ordinary,* 252.

26. Lash, *Easter in Ordinary,* 274.

27. Lash, *Easter in Ordinary,* 94.

28. Lash, *Easter in Ordinary,* 253.

CHAPTER SEVEN: THE MINISTER AS ARTIST

1. Quoted in Bede Griffiths, *The Golden String* (London: Fontana, 1964), 9.

2. See Kathryn Spink, *A Sense of the Sacred: A Biography of Bede Griffiths* (London: SPCK, 1988), 24.

3. George Every, *Something of Every-Man: A Celebration,* limited edition (Oscott, United Kingdom: Oscott Press, 1989).

4. Primo Levi, *The Drowned and the Saved* (New York: Vintage [Random House], 1989), 32.

5. Levi, *The Drowned,* 29.

6. Review of Studs Terkel's *The Great Divide: Second Thoughts on the American Dream* in the *Times Literary Supplement,* 17–23 February 1989.

7. See 2 Sam. 6:6 and 1 Chron. 13:9.

8. See V. S. Pritchett, *Chekhov: A Spirit Set Free* (New York: Random House, 1988).

9. Pritchett , *Chekhov,* 130–32.

10. Lewis Hyde, *The Gift: Imagination and the Erotic Life of Property* (New York: Vintage Books [Random House], 1983), iv.

11. Hyde, *The Gift,* xi–xiv.

12. Benjamin Hoff, *The Tao of Pooh* (New York: E. P. Dutton, 1982), viii–x.

13. Hoff, *The Tao of Pooh,* viii.

14. Iris Murdoch, *The Black Prince* (London: Chatto and Windus, 1973).

15. *Times Literary Supplement,* 3–9 March 1989, 220.

16. Clare Kirchberger, *Richard of St. Victor: Selected Writings on Contemplation* (London: Faber & Faber, 1957), 85.

17. Malcolm Muggeridge, *A Third Testament* (Boston: Little, Brown, 1976), 25.

18. Richard Wilhelm and C. G. Jung, *The Secret of the Golden Flower* (London: Kegan Paul, 1938), 129.

19. See Hyde, *The Gift,* 18.

20. Muggeridge, *A Third Testament,* 117.

21. Thomas Klise, *Last Western* (London: Argus, 1974), 159.

22. D. H. Lawrence, *Kangaroo* (New York: Viking Press, 1960), 36.

23. Auden's introduction to Eiseley's *The Star Thrower* (New York: Times Books, 1978), iv.

24. David Tracy, *The Analogical Imagination* (New York: Crossroad, 1981), 339.

25. Charles Williams, *Shadows of Ecstasy* (Grand Rapids, MI: William B. Eerdmans, 1973), 102–4.

CHAPTER EIGHT: THE MINISTER AS ACTOR

1. Edward Farley, "The Modernist Element in Protestantism," *Theology Today,* July 1990, 132.

2. Peter Brook, *The Empty Space* (London: Pelican, 1972), 54.

3. Brook, *The Empty Space,* 88.

4. Brook, *The Empty Space,* 65.

5. Brook, *The Empty Space,* 1.

6. Brook, *The Empty Space,* 66.

7. W. H. Auden, introduction to *The Protestant Mystics,* ed. Anne Fremantle (Boston: Little, Brown, 1964), 8.

8. Hermann Hesse, *My Belief* (New York: Farrar, Straus & Giroux, 1974), 62.

9. Brook, *The Empty Space,* 12.

10. Brook, *The Empty Space,* 42.

11. Brook, *The Empty Space,* 62.

12. Brook, *The Empty Space,* 79.

13. Brook, *The Empty Space,* 80.

14. Brook, *The Empty Space,* 100.

15. Brook, *The Empty Space,* 108–9.

16. Brook, *The Empty Space,* 121.

CHAPTER NINE: SACRIFICE

1. Raimundo Panikkar, *The Vedic Experience* (Berkeley: Univ. of California Press, 1977), 98.

2. Panikkar, *The Vedic Experience,* 93–94.

3. Norman Sherry, *The Life of Graham Greene,* vol. 1, 1904–1939 (New York: Viking, 1989), 699.

4. From a memoir by Tess Gallagher in *Granta,* no. 25 (London: Penguin, 1988), 167.

5. See *The Jewish Guide to the Here and Hereafter,* ed. Lionel Blue and Jonathan Magonot (New York: Crossroad, 1988), 118.

6. Nicholas Lash, *Easter in Ordinary* (Charlottesville: Univ. of Virginia Press, 1988), 222.

7. Karl Rahner, *The Practice of Faith: A Handbook of Contemporary Spirituality,* ed. Karl Lehman and Albert Raffelt (New York: Crossroad, 1983), 78.

8. A. N. Wilson, *The Healing Art* (London: Penguin, 1982).

9. Wilson, *The Healing Art,* 7.

10. Wilson, *The Healing Art,* 83.

11. Wilson, *The Healing Art,* 26–27.

12. Wilson, *The Healing Art,* 49.

13. Wilson, *The Healing Art,* 50.

14. Wilson, *The Healing Art,* 50.

15. Letter to author, May 1988.

16. Elizabeth Cogburn, personal communication.

17. Gregory Dix, *The Shape of the Liturgy* (London: A & C Black, 1945), 744.

18. C. S. Lewis, *The Weight of Glory and Other Addresses* (London: Geoffrey Bles, 1949).

CHAPTER TEN: DELIGHT

1. A phrase from Martin Heidegger.
2. MacManus, *The Greatest of These* (Cork, Ireland: Mercier Press, 1943), 19.
3. MacManus, *The Greatest of These,* 47.
4. Peter Brook, *The Empty Space* (London: Pelican, 1972), 81.

CHAPTER ELEVEN: SONG AND SUFFERING

1. Frederick Crews, "The Parting of the Twains," *New York Review of Books,* 20 July 1989.
2. Crews, "The Parting of the Twains," 39.
3. Crews, "The Parting of the Twains," 39.
4. "The Government of the Tongue," xiff.
5. Peter Brook, *The Empty Space* (London: Pelican, 1972), 51.
6. See Brook, *The Empty Space,* 51.
7. Brook, *The Empty Space,* 57.
8. Brook, *The Empty Space,* 52.
9. Primo Levi, *The Drowned and the Saved* (New York: Vintage [Random House], 1989), 69.

CHAPTER TWELVE: MAKING ONE FAMILY

1. Murdoch, *The Book and the Brotherhood* (New York: Viking, 1988), 63.
2. Murdoch, *The Book and the Brotherhood,* 302–4.
3. Quoted in Nicholas Lash, *Easter in Ordinary* (Charlottesville: Univ. of Virginia Press, 1988), 203.
4. Lash, *Easter in Ordinary,* 212.
5. See Thomas Nagel's review of Alasdair McIntyre's *Whose Justice? Which Rationality?* in *Times Literary Supplement,* 8–14 July 1988, 747.
6. Nagel review, 749.
7. Meriol Trevor, *Light in Winter* (London: Macmillan, 1962), 5. (This is the second volume in the two-volume biography entitled *Newman.*)
8. See Polanyi in *Personal Knowledge* (New York: Harper & Row, 1964), 29–30.
9. See Gabriel Josipovici's review of Milan Kundera's book in the *Times Literary Supplement,* 24–30 June 1988, 695ff.
10. Murdoch, *The Book and the Brotherhood,* 179.
11. Murdoch, *The Book and the Brotherhood,* 135.
12. Murdoch, *The Book and the Brotherhood,* 136.
13. Murdoch, *The Book and the Brotherhood,* 135–36.
14. Murdoch, *The Book and the Brotherhood,* 137.
15. Murdoch, *The Book and the Brotherhood,* 376.

16. Michael Ignatieff, *The Needs of Strangers* (New York: Penguin, 1986).
17. Ignatieff, *The Needs of Strangers*, 13.
18. Ignatieff, *The Needs of Strangers*, 30.
19. Ignatieff, *The Needs of Strangers*, 28.
20. Ignatieff, *The Needs of Strangers*, 37.
21. Ignatieff, *The Needs of Strangers*, 50.

EPILOGUE

1. From Simon Leys, "The Curse of the Man Who Could See the Little Fish at the Bottom of the Ocean," *New York Review of Books*, 20 July 1989, 29.
2. (New York: Viking Press, 1960), 166.
3. Rowan Williams, "Affirming Tradition," in *Affirming Catholicism,* papers given at a conference at St. Alban's Holborn, on Saturday, 9 June 1990, London, Mainsteam, St. Mary le Bow.
4. Elizabeth Jennings, *Collected Poems, 1953–1985* (New York: Carcanet Press, 1986/87).

Index